You Can Write Greeting Cards

KAREN ANN MOORE

WRITER'S DIGEST BOOKS
CINCINNATI, OHIO

Permissions

The greeting cards reproduced on the cover are used by permission of Current, Inc. © 1998 Current, Inc.

Artwork on page 31 is reproduced by permission of the Kersten Brothers. © 1998 Kersten Brothers.

The cartoon by Mike Peters appearing on page 93 is used by permission of Grimmy, Inc. © 1998 Grimmy, Inc.

Ziggy cartoons appearing on pages 9, 27, and 35 are reprinted by permission of Ziggy & Friends, Inc. © 1996 Ziggy & Friends, Inc. Ziggy is a registered trademark of Tom Wilson. Distributed by Universal Press Syndicate.

Other fine Writer's Digest Books are available from your local bookstore or direct from the publisher.

Visit our Web site at www.writersdigest.com for information on more resources for writers.

To receive a free biweekly E-mail newsletter delivering tips and updates about writing and about Writer's Digest products, send an E-mail with "Subscribe Newsletter" in the body of the message to newsletter-request@writersdigest.com, or register directly at our Web site at www.writersdigest.com.

03   02   01   00   99   5   4   3   2   1

Library of Congress Cataloging-in-Publication Data

Moore, Karen Ann
    You can write greeting cards / Karen Ann Moore.
      p.   cm.
    Includes index.
    ISBN 0-89879-824-8 (alk. paper)
    1. Greeting cards—Authorship. I. Title.
PN171.G74M66   1999
808'.02—dc21

98-31434
CIP

Editors: Jack Heffron and Barbara Kuroff
Production editor: Nicole R. Klungle
Designer: Sandy Conopeotis Kent
Cover designer: Mary Barnes Clark
Production coordinator: Erin Boggs

About the Author

Karen Ann Moore has been a professional greeting card writer and editor for nearly twenty years. She has worked for American Greetings Corporation, headed her own studio for writing and product development and served as a Creative Director for Gibson Greetings, Inc. Karen holds a master's degree in education and is a frequent speaker at writing conferences. She has published over two thousand greeting cards in her career. She has three children and makes her home in Colorado Springs.

Acknowledgments

I'd like to give my warmest thanks to the companies and the people who helped me with this book by providing moral support, artwork, ideas and inspiration. There are many such people and though I cannot list them all here, I appreciate the valuable input you all gave me. I expecially want to thank Gibson Greetings for copy ideas and the expertise of some of the most gifted writers and editors in the business. In that regard, I thank Tom Kapella, Larry Sandman, Holly Davis, Nancy Breen, Gary Morgan, Dick Lorenz, Angela Walsh, Cindy Duesing, Clare Kathmann, Dan Dunham and Megan Brown. I'd also like to thank my dear friend Debbie Paul of American Greetings. I'd like to thank Tom Wilson and Caroline Kenneth from Ziggy & Friends, Inc., Mike Peters from Grimmy, Inc., the Kersten Brothers and my friend Jackie Kersten, and Cathy Guisewite for their kind permission to use quotations and artwork. From Current, Inc. I'd like to thank Lee Meyer for his support, Jeanne Appleton for her encouragement, Tom Bowker for the photo on the dedication page, and Todd Hafer, Jonna Gress, Mar Porter and Elaine Myers for their individual help and support. I also thank my sister, Donna Ryan, for years of simply believing in me. Finally, or perhaps foremost, I'd like to thank Barb Kuroff for her encouragement, insights, and talent in helping bring this manuscript to light. Special thanks to Jack Heffron, who was instrumental in making the whole project possible. Thanks and love to all of you.

TABLE OF CONTENTS

INTRODUCTION

You probably picked up this book because you want to know more about writing greeting cards or you know someone who does. Or perhaps you're just curious. Hey, I think that's a good start.

Now, there are a couple things standing between you and the big money you can make in the greeting card business. First, you need to know the techniques for writing those verses—called sentiments—that make it onto the cards you see in the stores. Second, you have to know something about what goes on behind the doors of the greeting card publishing houses and just what it takes to get your stuff in the right person's hands.

The good news is that greeting card publishers really do look for freelancers. The ad on the next page, from Gibson Greetings in Cincinnati, Ohio, could have appeared in a number of publications across the country, especially in Cleveland, Kansas City and Cincinnati, where the top three greeting card publishers are headquartered. They are all in the market for fresh ideas and are just waiting for writers like you to provide them. So, if you've been thinking about trying your hand at this kind of writing, it's time to get started. After all, your future may be in the cards!

All You Need to Know

This book will teach you everything you need to know about writing and selling sentiments for greeting cards. You will learn what types of cards are published and who shops for them (your audience). You'll find out what's hot and what's not and what's really salable. If you frequently browse greeting card racks in the shopping mall

WRITE FUNNY GREETING CARDS AND MAKE MILLIONS
of people laugh!

Great Greetings, America's funniest greeting card maker, is paying $$ for great humorous card ideas. If you're a freelance writer or cartoonist with funny ideas (the printable kind) and you'd like to experience the thrill of seeing your work on greeting cards, (what kid doesn't dream of that!) send an S.A.S.E. to this guy for info:

Steve Martin
Humor Managing Editor
Great Greetings, Inc.
2000 Anystreet Rd.
P.O. Box 2001
Yourtown, OH 45000-2001

or grocery store, you're off to a good start. This book will help you move from your own consumer experience to the position of greeting card writer.

You also need to know how the industry is evolving. It is easier now than ever before to get your work into an editor's hands because fresh, new and innovative material is in high demand. If you're ready to offer *new* direction, *new* suggestions and *new* approaches for markets, the time couldn't be better for you to get into this business.

How Do You Develop Your Idea?

The examples and illustrations used in this book will show you a bit of what has worked in the past, some of what you need to think about in the present and a glimpse of what will work in the future—that's where your consumers are going to be. I've asked some freelancers and in-house writers to offer you advice about what works and what to submit. Read what these experts share and then play the "what if" game. What if you come up with an innovative approach? What if you think of a niche that isn't currently being addressed? What if you try a writing style new to greeting card publishers? What if you challenge the thinking of the in-house experts? What if? . . . Read on and fill in the blanks yourself.

Study the cards on the market and go a few steps further. What isn't being done? What don't you find that you really want? How would you want to see your card line merchandised? What would you want it to communicate? What would you want the card to be made of? What should it cost? What art style would you choose for your card line? How do you want to buy a greeting card? Do you want the card shop to feel like a coffee shop so you can really take time to browse? Do you want to be entertained as you shop? Do you like interactive cards? This book will help you answer these questions. It will give you the tools you need to get in the door of the best publishers and to make sales in the months and years ahead.

Still Looking for You!

Greeting card publishers have a great need for creative input from talented writers like you because their needs continue to change. In-house writers are busy with the daily needs of traditional markets and often don't have the time to create new markets. You have an advantage as a freelancer because, as a consumer, you know more about what consumers need and want. You can see the trends and the fads and respond to them. You can do the necessary research. Go ahead, do your homework! It will pay off—right in your mailbox. Let's take a look at the past and the present and then move into the future. The industry needs you more than ever! We're all anxious for you to get started.

1 THE INDUSTRY

The greeting card industry as a whole has experienced little growth in sales and market categories recently. Some cards first printed over twenty years ago are still on the racks today. In a recent study, I found cards with copy and art identical to cards published ten years before. The only differences were color changes and pricing.

Major card publishers have pretty reliable rating systems that tell them that certain ideas sell well to every generation of card buyers. These ideas are considered *classic* and are used over and over again. For instance, one classic card shows a cute character on the front saying, "Know how much I love you?" The card opens to show the character with arms stretched wide, exclaiming, "This much!" This card has the kind of appeal that will make it sell consistently over time. Though the classics will continue to sell in the future, more innovative ideas are the hot topic of the day—and that's why publishers are interested in you.

A Brief Look Back

Greeting card manufacturers once produced cards that were more complex and intricate in design than many that are published now. The cost of producing fancy cards with lace inserts and intricate die cuts (cutouts) and folds prohibits most companies from making them today. However, the popularity of handmade cards or those that have a handmade *feel* are an indication that we shouldn't necessarily avoid old-fashioned looks. In this high-tech, fast-paced world, consumers and publishers still wish to respect and preserve a feeling of heritage and the "specialness" of hand-made items. Ideas that people can relate to from their own past always sell in greeting cards, so looks and sentiment ideas that celebrated past events are often published again.

Nostalgia is always trendy and should be considered when you're looking for series ideas. If we had a photograph of an old card shop from the 1950s, we might see the same tired card racks and displays still found in local malls and supermarkets. Well, hold on to your MTV, because a new era in social expression is about to begin. Gibson Greetings, for instance, has developed an innovative approach. In the words of the CEO, Gibson is in the *entertainment* business, not the *greeting card* business.

You may have noticed from your own recent shopping experiences that an effort is being made to make shopping more fun. Card racks in grocery stores and discount stores have become more like small shops within the bigger store environment. This is meant to draw you to the rack and is sure to have an impact on the market, the industry and therefore on all of us who work in it. Writers will have to keep up with consumer trends in the marketplace in order to know what to submit to publishing houses.

A History of Greeting Cards

The historical perspective varies from publisher to publisher, but the basic scenario is something like this. If you wanted to send a card in the 1840s, you went to your local dry goods store and told the clerk you'd like to send a message. He pulled out a book of sentiments you could copy, or offered some printed in beautiful calligraphy you could insert into a blank card.

Sometime in the 1870s, calendar maker Louis Prang found a better way to make cards. He pasted sentiments on some old calendar art (with little regard for whether the text and art matched), and became the first to mass-produce greeting cards. For his time, this was a pretty innovative thing to do. Somehow he managed to make Christmas cards out of sailboat art.

5

By the early 1900s, J.C. Hall and Jacob Saperstein were out with their pushcarts selling greeting cards on street corners. People liked the convenience of these new greeting cards, and Hallmark and American Greetings were born. Card sales increased greatly with the advent of World War I, when keeping in touch became extremely important. By the time of the Great Depression, people had grown used to greeting cards and purchased cards printed on wallpaper, paper bags, paper towels and other cheap substances. American Greetings still publishes a paper bag card as a reminder of those times.

World War II created high demand for cards for servicemen and servicewomen, and the greeting card industry grew as a consequence, and nonoccasion cards emerged. Coming out of the War, a more cynical nation developed what became known as the studio card. These cards answered the needs of the educated consumer who didn't think the world was quite as rose-colored as it had once seemed. Cards were produced with uplifting messages like, "You want to lose ten ugly pounds . . . cut off your head!" Here's another old favorite: "Candy is dandy . . . but sex won't rot your teeth!"

The 1960s brought Vietnam and a market full of young girls waiting for their boyfriends to come home. The cute "thinking of you" kinds of cards evolved as part of the daily correspondence between these girls and their sweethearts in Vietnam. During the *Love Story* era of the 1970s, cards became softer and more romantic. There was a definite return to optimism and a belief that the "sun would come out tomorrow." Tom Wilson was busy creating that lovable loser, Ziggy, and at about this time, Irving Stone, the son of Jacob Saperstein and founder of American Greetings, discovered a young woman named Holly while visiting England. When Holly married Donald Hobbie, Holly Hobbie was born and became a memorable character mimicked for years by others across the industry. This was the era of those huge hippo cards that cost five dollars and simply said "I love you"; these were swept up by the young at heart who bought them as gifts as well as cards.

The trends of the 1980s, the era of the energy crisis and inflation, reflected a more realistic approach to greeting cards. Reality had to be faced, and cards for people dealing with divorce, quitting drinking or smoking, and other life issues were generated.

The 1990s have seen an increased trend to nonoccasion cards, encouragement cards and longer, prose, heart-to-heart style copy. Consumers became ready to communicate in real ways. In this generation of single-parent families, nonoccasion cards were developed for kids to encourage them in difficult situations. Humor and romance have followed more realistic attitudes about relationships, as well. Here's a closer look at what's going on today.

Current Trends

Some of the present trends have been noted by Faith Popcorn, who wrote *The Popcorn Report*, and more recently, *Clicking*. We also read books that discuss religious, sports and global trends, as well as the works of John Naisbit and Patricia Aburdene, who brought us *Megatrends* and *Megatrends 2000*. Trend researchers and greeting card publishers check sources like the *Yanklovich Monitor*, *American Demographics* and magazines like *Gifts and Decorative Accessories* and *Giftware News*. These sources help greeting card companies to know their consumers, so each year the trend gurus are consulted to forecast what's ahead. A few of the more notable consumer trends from some of these sources lead us to believe that consumers

- make their homes more comfortable places in order to avoid the outside world. *(Could this mean more cards will be purchased on the Internet and through catalogs?)*
- share interests or hobbies in places such as bookstores, coffee houses and exercise clubs. *(What other places will people gather to connect with those around them?)*
- look for adventure in computer games, science fiction movies and fighter pilot simulators. *(What does this need say about our otherwise quiet lives?)*
- disregard feelings of guilt when they eat hot fudge sundaes, hamburgers or real whipped cream. *(Aren't we getting tired of feeling guilty about everything we do?)*
- buy affordable little luxuries for themselves or for their homes. *(Maybe I'm surrounded by debt, but I deserve something special to show for my hard work!)*
- seek broader awareness of spiritual things. *(I really don't want to be alone in the world.)*

- desire to be seen as unique and special. *(Whether I'm younger, older, skilled or unskilled, I am uniquely me.)*
- want to connect with others in more significant ways. *(Let's talk to each other. Want to join me in a chat room?)*
- appreciate kinder, gentler, but still strong men. *(It's OK to cry at movies and be emotionally available, guys. We like all people to be nurturing.)*
- feel somewhat overwhelmed by responsibilities. *(Stop the world. I want to get off . . . at least for a while.)*
- like alternative medicines and holistic health. *(Can't I take care of this illness without drugs?)*
- don't want to be categorized or labeled. *(Don't call me a Gen-Xer or a Senior. I'm special!)*
- assume no loyalties either from or to corporations. *(It's an outsourcing, downsizing world in corporate America. There are no guarantees.)*
- question the belief systems of former generations. *(It's a wonderfully diverse world and I want to be part of it.)*
- are genuinely interested in caring for the environment. *(Will Mother Earth still be there to take care of my children?)*

Keep these lifestyle trends in mind, and you'll have a better sense of what consumers want in a greeting card.

 IDEA
JOGGER

Turn any of the lifestyle trends just discussed into a greeting card situation. If your idea is conventional, make it humorous. If it's funny, make it into a tearjerker. Life is full of emotions. Greeting card writers help to communicate those emotions.

Tom Wilson's cartoon below depicting Ziggy at the card rack is a fun example of the way greeting cards become categorized. I don't think we actually have a thank-you-for-your-card-that-thanked-me-for-my-card-to-you card, but hey, it could be an idea.

Greeting Card Trends to Keep in Mind
- Interest continues for cards that can also serve as gifts.
- Photography is finding a greater acceptance.
- Meaningful prose and topical situations are being addressed by more publishers.
- Animals are always good subject matter.

- There is an interest in cards that are religious or motivational.
- Romance and friendship cards are stronger.
- Generation Xers do send greeting cards.
- Over one billion birthday cards are sold annually.
- Humorous cards are growing in popularity.
- The most popular adult milestone birthday is forty.
- The percentage of older people in the general population is increasing.
- There is a trend back to traditional family values.

2 ARE YOU A GREETING CARD WRITER?

Do you browse card racks, reading funny cards or the emotional heart-warmers and think to yourself, "I could have written that"? How about that card you wrote for your friend because you couldn't find what you wanted? How about that card you bought for your mother, but still added your own message because it didn't quite say the right thing? Are you always particular about the cards you pick out? If you answer yes to any of these questions, you might be ready to join the social expression industry as a freelance greeting card writer.

Social Expression and the Greeting Card Industry

Social expression is how you express yourself to others in everyday relationships. You relate to lots of people each day. Your natural desire to communicate, to reach out, to console and to share life's ups and downs is what the greeting card business is all about.

The reason for this book is to show you what the industry is looking for, how you can write the sentiments they want, how to get your foot in the door, and provide a few tips that will help you be a successful freelancer. People like you are an important part of shaping the greeting card products of today.

This is kind of a "chicken or the egg" concept. Do relationships drive our need to create new products in greeting cards, or do greeting cards provide a way for us to develop new relationships? Perhaps it's a bit of both. As you consider greeting card ideas, keep this thought in mind.

What Kind of Background Do You Need to Write Greeting Cards?

The best greeting cards are written by people with a variety of backgrounds and interests. A degree in English or experience as a stand-up comic may or may not make you a profitable greeting card writer. What you need, more than the right degree, is an accurate understanding of people. You need to be intuitive and sensitive on one hand, and outrageous, funny and clever on the other. You need to be a student of life, an observer of all kinds of situations and a willing communicator.

The best greeting card writers have a world view that helps them understand more or laugh more at the ways people relate to each other. They're not afraid to try new things, to play with ideas, to stretch their thinking a little further. Sometimes, they're people who've kept journals or who've written poetry, or they're loyal fans of Letterman or *Saturday Night Live*. Teachers, moms, attorneys and researchers become greeting card writers. What you bring to the industry will come from what *you* know, and what you know may be just the ticket to success.

How Do You Get Started?

I believe you need to have a sense of your market before you can write effectively. Therefore, it makes sense to precede our discussion of how to write with a discussion of how to know your market. For me, it's always helpful to have an idea of the material publishers may want so I have a place to start. You may not understand all the terminology when you do the marketplace search, but most of it will be clear by the time you're finished with this book.

One excellent reference that will help you get started is the annual *Writer's Market*; check the listing under "Greeting Cards & Gift Ideas." Recent editions have offered a wealth of information on publishers and current needs. Some publishers will give you an idea of what they are looking for, and others will ask you to send for writer's guidelines. I strongly suggest that you do so. The more information you can get from the publisher, the better your odds of being published. Always be sure to send your SASE (self-addressed stamped envelope) when you request guidelines. Attention to details is what marks you as a professional.

Here's the listing for Paramount Cards, Inc. from the *Writer's Market* for 1996.

Paramount Cards, Inc., Dept. WM, P.O. Box 6546, Providence, RI 02940-6546. (401) 726-0800. Contact: Editorial Freelance Coordinator. Estab. 1906. Buys 100s of ideas/year. *(This is good for you to know. It tells you whether it's worth submitting ideas to them. Obviously, the more cards the company buys per year, the better the odds that you'll have success.)* **Submit seasonal material 1 month in advance.** *(Actually, this seasonal note is a bit surprising because most companies work on seasons several months in advance and often over a year ahead of the actual selling season.)* **Reports in 1 month.** *(One month is not bad. It's not much fun to submit to companies that do not return your material for several months. No one should take over two months without explaining the reason for the delay.)* **Buys all rights.** *(This means that you cannot sell this card again. The company now owns it as though they wrote it in-house. We'll look at copyright information in a later chapter.)* **Pays on acceptance.** *(This is important to you because you might find it rather disheartening to have to wait for a payment until your card idea is actually published.)* **Writer's Guidelines for SASE.** *(OK, do this part. It only costs you a couple stamps and will save you a lot of headaches.)* **NEEDS:** *(This is where you find the current needs for each publisher.)* **All types of conventional verses. Fresh, inventive humorous verses, especially family birthday cards.** *(Believe me, they want you to be fresh and inventive in your conventional rhymes too.)* **Would also like to see more conversational prose, especially in family titles such as Mother, Father, Sister, Husband, Wife, etc.** *(It makes sense that you're going to want personal messages in family and love captions.)* **Submit 10–15/batch.** *(It is typical to send ten to fifteen, but sometimes you can send more. You need to have a good system for keeping track, and we'll look at system ideas in a later chapter.)* **No tired, formulaic rhymes.** *(Don't send any version of* *"roses are red, violets are blue" or other formulas.)* **TIPS:** *(This could be the most helpful part. Read the tips carefully.)* **Study the market! Go to your local card shops and analyze what you see. Ask the storekeepers which cards are selling. Then apply what you've learned to your own writing. The best cards (and we buy only the best) will have mass appeal and yet, in the consumer's eyes, will read as though they were created exclusively for her. A feminine touch is important as 90 percent of all greeting cards are purchased by women.**

These listings are excellent tools and will give you a better understanding of what the market expects. The greeting card section of *Writer's Market* has added many new publishers. The industry has definitely grown. There are well over fifteen hundred greeting card publishers.

Are They Really Looking for More Greeting Card Writers?

The big three card makers—Hallmark, American Greetings and Gibson Greetings—have a continuing need for fresh and new ideas, and that's where you come in. They know you might send ideas they already own or some that just would not work, but you also might send a gem that they wouldn't have otherwise seen. Beyond the big three are hundreds of smaller publishers who rely heavily on the talents of freelancers. They don't have the luxury of in-house writing staffs and have a constant need for freelance writers (at least until their yearly budget dries up, so find out up front the date their fiscal year begins).

What About the Publishers?

Generally, the big three companies will review humor submissions, even if they don't take conventional freelance. However, many companies will not accept cold submissions. Most will require a signed disclosure form before they'll look at your work. This form states that you're writing original material and you give the company permission to review and possibly purchase your work. It protects you and the publisher if there is any disagreement about rights. Publishers will probably review your submissions for some time before sending you a specific assignment until they get to know your style and remember it. When that happens, the editor will usually do a "call for entries" (a request for submissions) on a particular topic or may just send you a specific assignment—to write juvenile Christmas cards, for example. An assignment request will come with a limited time frame and a rate that you'll be paid for the work.

If you sell consistently to a publisher and like the way they return your submissions in a reasonable time, you might want to approach them about a contract. A freelance contract can be a good thing because you can expect a certain income from your writing, but it can be a limitation. Contracts are generally based on a quota of written material accepted by the publisher in a given time period. Freelance contracts are offered in a number of ways. Some publishers will want your work to be exclusive to them, however, so make sure it's beneficial for you to write for only one company before you sign a contract.

A Little Greeting Card Glossary

You need to have an industry-useful vocabulary. Let's look at the terms you may not be familiar with.

Caption: The big greeting card manufacturers generally publish several hundred cards centered around the same occasion. These are broken down into programs called captions. Any given caption program will offer a variety of product types. It may be the birthday, wedding/anniversary, get well, sympathy, friendship, baby, love, Christmas, Halloween, Thanksgiving, Valentine's Day, Easter, St. Patrick's Day, Sweetest Day, Grandparents Day, Secretaries Day, Boss's Day, Father's Day or Mother's Day line. Within each caption group, you will find specific intended recipients. *Caption* is also used to identify the words that address the recipient of a card, such as "My Sister, My Friend" or "For You, Mother."

Construction: We think about how a sentiment is put together when we consider its construction. How is it built? Is it composed of one line of copy that seems to fit the artwork? Is it two lines that rhyme and form a couplet? Does it have three rhyme lines or four? Is it a fairly long paragraph that doesn't rhyme? Is the prose short or medium length? Is there any kind of pattern to the prose (known as structured prose)? Does it have alliteration or strong imagery or offer a wordplay? Does it focus on one specific idea or offer a variety of topics to consider? The construction is very important to the mood or the tone of the piece you're writing. Sometimes a sentiment that intends to sound like someone is speaking directly from the heart works better in prose. Other times, a silly humorous piece is more fun in rhyme. If we think of the construction as a car, for instance, then the content determines whether the car is a jalopy or a luxury sedan.

Conventional cards: Many companies define their cards in categories. Generally the two major divisions are everyday and seasonal. Everyday conventional cards are traditional in their approaches to non-holiday events (such as birthdays). We usually call them conventional if they aren't humorous or alternative in their approach. Seasonal cards, of course, reflect on a particular season of the year and utilize a wide variety of themes.

Imagery: Imagery refers to any words in the sentiment that create a picture in your mind. Knowing the artwork is calling for a sentiment about puppies or birthdays or food may be helpful to the editor searching on a computerized retrieval system for a verse that might be used again. Strong imagery works well in humor, but may also help sell a conventional sentiment. Classic sympathy pieces, like "The Rose Beyond the Wall" or those that incorporate bridges or gates to heaven, rely heavily on images.

Meter: The most often used metric forms are iambic, trochaic, anapestic and dactylic. The meter refers to the number of beats per line and which syllables are emphasized. Iambic is used most often in greeting cards and follows a pattern of an unstressed syllable and then one or more stressed syllables. We refer to these syllable pairs as feet, and a typical verse moves from four metric feet in the odd-numbered lines to three metric feet in the even-numbered lines. Thus a typical verse (using — as the stressed syllable and ‿ as the unstressed syllable) looks like this:

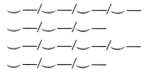

For example:

> *Here's hoping that your birthday, Sis,*
> *Brings happiness your way,*
> *'Cause you deserve the nicest things*
> *On your most special day!*

Trochaic meter is the opposite of iambic in that it consists of an accented syllable followed by an unaccented one: —⌣/—⌣/ —⌣/—⌣.

This verse uses trochaic in the first and third lines and iambic in the second and fourth:

> *Wishing you a day of sunshine,*
> *with special joys all through it, . . .*
> *Hoping that you'll soon be well*
> *and that there's nothing to it!*

Most verses follow one of these two patterns, though often not strictly. The two other useful greeting card meters are anapestic (which is two unaccented syllables followed by an accented one) and dactylic (which is the reverse of that). Here are a couple examples:

Anapestic:

> *It's a pleasure to have*
> *a dear friend like you;*
> *It's so fun to think back*
> *on the things we've been through,*
> *And it's nice to remind you*
> *that all through the year,*
> *You're especially loved*
> *And especially dear!*

Dactylic:

> *All that brings happiness,*
> *All that brings cheer,*

That's what you're wished
Through a wonderful year!

These two meters are used to give a light, happy feeling to a verse and are good directions to go when you're getting bogged down in the more traditional styles. Learning to use these approaches may increase your sales.

Occasion: The occasion is the event the card addresses. Is it for a birthday, Christmas, St. Patrick's Day or no particular event at all? The occasions asked for the most are birthday, friendship, get well, sympathy, congratulations, wedding/anniversary, baby and a variety of smaller ones. We call these everyday occasions. These are the events that can occur at any time throughout the year and, therefore, are needed the most. Other occasions, called seasonal, are those that deal with specific holidays. Seasonal cards for Christmas, Valentine's Day, Mother's Day, Father's Day, Easter and graduation are the most often requested.

Pages: Greeting cards are said to have pages, and they are numbered according to the type of fold the card has. In general, page one is the outside of the card. Page two is the immediate inside left; page three, the inside right; and page four, the back. It's helpful to know this, because your copy could appear on any one of these pages. The most popular folds are single folds, with or without extra paper (verse inserts), French folds, tri-folds (also called Z- or 3-folds), gatefolds, barrel folds and short folds (some of these are shown on the next page). The paging differs on all of these. With so many types of folds, it helps to ask your editors if they know what format will be used for the cards you're writing.

Price point: It often helps you to know the price of a card because the more expensive a card is, typically the bigger it is, and the more room there is for copy. An expensive card will usually have more pages and more finishes. (A finish is the term for such special effects as embossing or foil.) As cards go up in size, they generally go up in price. However, square cards and other trendy, less conventional shapes may be smaller while actually costing more because of their unique die cuts.

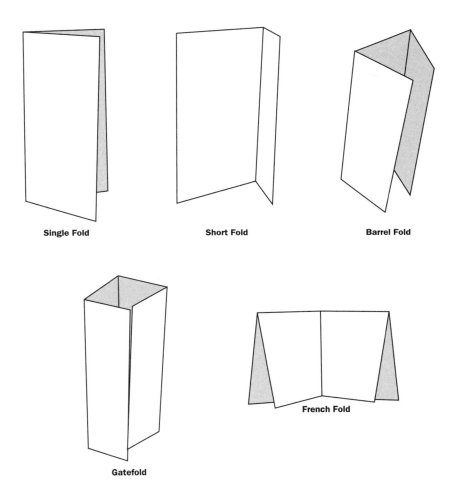

Single Fold

Short Fold

Barrel Fold

Gatefold

French Fold

Prose: Prose refers to the form used most often when you want to speak directly to the recipient in a very conversational me-to-you style. It does not rhyme, but may have structure (such as a refrain line like, "I love you because . . ."). It may have a cadence, almost like rhyme, effected by word choices and the use of alliteration. If it has a refrain line, a repeated line or a recognizable pattern, we call it structured prose.

Quote: A quote is additional copy on a card. It does not have a me-to-you message and is meant to give extra information or emphasis to

19

a sentiment or to the artwork used on a card. It may be anything from a Bible verse to a literary quote from *Bartlett's Familiar Quotations* to a special piece you wrote about what it means to be a mother. Strong additional copy pieces are an important part of greeting card writing and a real opportunity for freelancers. Quotes can be more poetic than a sentiment because they aren't usually trying to establish a personal connection to the reader.

Recipient: The recipient is the person/persons who will receive the card. Will it go to a son, a grandfather, a sweetheart, an old friend or a couple celebrating their anniversary?

Relationship: The relationship identifies how close the recipient and the sender are to each other. Are they friends, soul mates or simply acquaintances? This is the key to what kind of card you will write. Relationships have levels of closeness or intimacy. Try to determine the range of possible relationships two people might have. For instance, when you think of someone as a friend, he might be a brand-new friend, an old high school friend, a best friend, a bowling friend or a shopping friend. The depth of the relationship will make a difference in the kind of card you write. As you are writing, imagine a person your sentiment could be for and create your ideas based on a variety of possible relationship levels.

Rhyme: If you like rhyming and it comes fairly easily for you, then rhyme may be a natural style for you to develop. Contrary to what you may think or how good writers make it appear, good rhyme is not easy to come by in greeting cards. As an editor, I have turned down many good ideas for rhymed verse that didn't stay consistent throughout the piece or didn't offer enough imagery for the artist to work with to make the card complete. New writers often try to put too many ideas into one card. By that, I mean that they start in one place and end up in a totally different or illogical place. They might begin a sentiment by talking about shoes and what their favorite colors are and end it by talking about kids. My advice here is to read your long verse aloud and make sure it holds together all the way through. The hardest thing is to make sure that you offer the reader the same smooth transitions you would if you were writing sentences in a letter or a story. Remember, even in a greeting card, the reader can only make the leaps in logic that you provide. Logic problems lead to rejection. Make sure every word has a reason for being in your card and that every word is meaningful.

Sender: The sender is the person sending the card. Is it being sent by one person, a child, two persons, a sister, a parent or a group? Try to imagine all the possible senders of a card. What would you as the sender be looking for?

Tag line: Generally an added piece of copy that leaves the recipient with a wish or extra thought, like "Happy Birthday" or "Congratulations" or "Enjoy Your Day." Sometimes this is the only real me-to-you portion of the card.

Theme: The theme is the main idea of the sentiment. Greeting card verses are usually judged by the limitation that a given phrase may put on a card. "Love" is a limiting theme because it implies that a particular kind of relationship exists between the sender and the receiver. "Memories" is also a limiting theme because it implies that the sender and recipient have known each other for quite some time.

Some of the most useful greeting card themes that will help focus your ideas are

- *General wishes*—wishes for the day, for happiness, life's good things, all the best.
- *Love/affection*—may refer to romantic love or love between friends, a wish for love in someone's life, or just a wish to send a hug.
- *Appreciation or gratitude*—"thanks for all you've done, for being you, for kindness, for your help, for caring."
- *How much you mean*—identifies an important relationship and expresses in real terms how much the recipient means to the sender.
- *Memories*—may involve shared memories or a wish to recall favorite memories.
- *Thinking of you*—expresses the thought that the recipient is on the sender's mind, in the sender's heart or in the sender's thoughts and prayers.
- *Missing you* or *wish you were here*—implies distance, either physical or emotional.
- *Sharing*—uses the word *share* to discuss shared activities or the desire to share time together.

21

- *Compliments*—uses expressions that define the recipient according to how special, kind, thoughtful, loving, etc., she is.
- *Advice*—generally tries to tell the recipient what to do in a given situation. It may be soft advice such as "enjoy your birthday" or more pointed advice like "you really need to get on with your life."
- *Religious themes (prayer, blessings, etc.)*—Helen Steiner Rice became one of the best-known greeting card writers ever by writing to religious and inspirational themes. Writers usually use light themes like hope, blessings and prayers, or heavier themes that literally speak of having God in your life.
- *Can't say it/don't say it*—"I have trouble telling you how I feel" or "I don't tell you often enough how I feel."
- *Nonsense*—This is just a silly card with no real message— think of *The Far Side*. These usually have a wish tag line of some kind.
- *I care about you*—expresses real warmth and concern for the person.
- *Gift*—the major reason for the card is to talk about the gift the recipient is not getting (especially in humor). Includes money cards.
- *Get well*—may be for short-term or serious illness; sometimes called cheer cards.
- *Apology/sorry*—the sender may regret something or express sympathy for something the recipient is going through.
- *Question or query*—These cards address a specific topic like "What is a friend?" and the copy goes on to describe what a friend is.
- *Statement*—a device that simply declares a fact, such as, "Today's your birthday!" There may be an added tag line.
- *Sympathy*—expression of sorrow over the loss of a loved one.
- *Toast/drinking*—"Here's to you and your success, graduation, new venture, etc."
- *Congratulations*—"Bravo, you did a great job!"
- *Encouragement*—"Keep trying. I know you can do it. I believe in you."

As you work with one company or another, you may find some variation in terminology, but these are fairly standard definitions. Themes can be used combined or alone in greeting card sentiments. Most cards have a primary theme, which is usually the most limiting, and then one or more secondary themes.

Type: Type refers to the kind of card you're being asked to write. Is it juvenile (meant to be for or from kids), traditional (meaning fairly expected or conventional in its approach to life or the specific occasion), religious (most likely with a Christian or Jewish slant), humorous, or cute (probably featuring some sweet-faced child or little kitten)?

Understanding Degrees of Intimacy

If you've had a date, a significant relationship, a child or an irritating sibling, you know something about intimacy. In greeting card writing, it's important to keep in mind that every occasion has a variety of possible relationships to be addressed within it. We usually think of the levels of possible relationships in terms of degrees of intimacy. How close are you to the person you want to receive that card? How much do you stay in touch? What is the depth of the relationship you share? Even within families levels of relationships exist. To help you with this idea, let's think about some of the roles you may play. If you're female, then you may be a sister, a daughter, a mother, a girlfriend, a wife, a sweetheart or a best friend. If you're male, then you may be a husband, a father, a brother, a boyfriend, a son or a grandfather. This should help you recognize the need for the many relationships that greeting card companies address.

Let's go back a minute and examine the female role possibilities. The occasion you have to consider is a birthday and the recipient is a sister. Think about either your own or other sisterly relationships, and imagine the types of emotional levels you might need to address. You need sister-to-sister, brother-to-sister, stepsister and like-a-sister ideas. Within those you should include everything from a very close loving relationship to one that is merely a form of obligation.

Example: Here's a nice, loving sister card in structured prose that offers a wish without going into a lot about the relationship itself.

23

Wishing you the kind of birthday   (occasion)
you'll remember with happiness,   (the wish)
because you're the kind of sister   (relationship)
who's always remembered with love.   (theme is love)

Now here's another prose example that is much more limiting in its sendability (that is, how many people could send it) because it offers some specifics about the sister that might not apply to *all* sisters.

Today I'm remembering so many special things
you've done that really make a difference in my life . . .
like the times you've encouraged me when I was
doubting myself, times you've helped me see
the funny side of a serious situation, and times
you've reached out even before I admitted
I needed someone. . . .
And I like to think I've made a difference
in your life, too, because I guess that's
what being sisters is all about.
                Happy Birthday

Now you should have a better understanding of the terminology and the types of greeting cards you can write to make sales. Greeting cards used to focus on "ideal" relationships, that is, all mothers would sound like saints and every relationship would sound perfect. That is no longer true. Most companies strive for a balance of compliments in the way they address family and friendship relationships. You no longer have to write sentiments that sound like mother was always there or every memory you have was of some perfect situation. It's no longer simply a rose-colored glasses kind of world. That should make your job as a writer a bit easier because you really can write from the heart. Just remember that a balance of idealism, realism and positive attitude will probably achieve the best results as you write your sentiments.

IDEA JOGGER

Your assignment is to write a traditional Dad birthday card with a long rhyme and assuming a close relationship between the sender and receiver. It should be a counter card, that is, on the card rack any time through the year as opposed to a summer card promotion or a specialty line that's only out for a short time. Jot down what you should think about to do this assignment, such as "things I remember Dad did for me as I was growing up," "things I admire about Dad," "wishes or compliments I might extend to Dad." Here's a good example of a card that would complete the above assignment.

CAPTION: TO A GREAT DAD

SENTIMENT:

Just looking back with love today on special memories—
The times I really needed your advice . . .
The strong support you've always been
Through changes in my life,
Your many gifts of willing sacrifice . . .
The good example that you set in quiet, thoughtful ways
That I understand much better since I'm grown . . .
And most of all, remembering
the friend you've always been,
The wise and patient love
you've always shown.

Happy Birthday, Dad!

Did you recognize the themes of love, memories, "how much you mean" and even advice?

Though the occasions will differ, the basic approach to writing greeting cards always remains the same. You are attempting to be the voice of ten thousand people at once. Without you and the words you provide, that voice might not be heard. You must be warm and personal, talk like you're saying something fresh and new and then do it in such a way that thousands of people will sign the card as though they wrote the words. Tom Wilson, the creator of the beloved character Ziggy, offers this thought about greeting card writing.

> A greeting card writer is ghostwriting for the consumer. Consumers are the ultimate judge of whether a card is good or not. They exercise that judgment in the most subjective and complimentary way—a purchase that they sign their name to, thereby making the words their own. The most important piece of copy is one we don't write—it's the consumer's signature inside the card.

Trends

Before we leave this introductory chapter, let's talk a little about the importance of trends to the greeting card industry and to you as a writer. Keeping ahead of the trends is as important to greeting cards as it is to fashion, home decor or publishing in general. Greeting card publishers try to keep up with trends by asking a number of important questions regarding various influences on popular culture.

- What's the top rated TV show? Top rated movie? What can we learn from the entertainment industry?
- What magazines draw the most readers? What books are on the top ten list?
- What are the color palettes for home decor?
- What are the top impulse items in the gift industry?
- What toys are getting the most attention?
- Is it a political year? What government issues will affect the industry or the marketplace?
- Is there a particular subject or object that you find in the market over and over again? For example, did you notice the flood of angels in the market in the past few years? What caused that trend? How long will it last? What will take its place?

Reprinted by permission of Ziggy & Friends, Inc. © 1996 Ziggy & Friends, Inc. Ziggy ® by Tom Wilson. Distributed by Universal Press Syndicate.

- What's happening to postal rates? Phone rates? Card rates? What does it cost to communicate?
- What are the music trends? Art trends?
- How do demographics affect trends? How big is the Generation X market segment? What's happening to baby boomers? What is the next marketing group that should be targeted?
- What are current consumers like? This question alone requires constant study and research.
- How will on-line greeting cards effect card sales in the future?

I could go on with this list, but you get the idea. It's important to keep up with as many aspects of the marketplace as you can. In the greeting card industry a few trends are notable.

- Cards are more expensive. (I bet you noticed that already.)
- A wider range of types of relationships is being addressed (stepparent, gay, close friends considered family, etc.).
- A wider range of subjects is being addressed (divorce, stress, coming out).
- Humorous cards have a harsher, more cynical approach to life.
- Smaller niche markets are being developed.
- Family relationships are being addressed in new ways.
- More spiritual views are being expressed.

 IDEA JOGGER

How can knowing the trends help you focus your writing for a specific kind of sentiment? Write some key words that will help you remember to tie into a current trend or topic.

Will You Get Rich and Famous in This Business?

Well, you might! The range of compensation for writing is generally divided between conventional writing and humorous writing. Compensation for conventional writing typically ranges from ten to two hundred dollars a verse. The fees paid are not really dependent on the length of your copy, but an unusually long piece may draw more compensation.

Humor writing usually brings more of the green stuff. You'll get anywhere from thirty-five to three hundred dollars. Of course, the larger amounts are generally drawn from the bigger publishers, but opportunity abounds. Some publishers will also pay you for offering them a variation on an idea they already have. Sometimes they'll pay you for giving them a glimmer of an idea that they develop more fully themselves. Typically, they'll pay some nominal fee for variations and glimmers, but it's still worth your time and effort. Greeting card publishers seldom offer royalties for your writing, however. Please understand that the compensation ranges for greeting card writing change all the time. Be sure to check with each publisher about their current compensation structure.

Beyond the real dollars, you'll enjoy the process of creating and becoming a spokesperson for a world growing by leaps and bounds in the information age. You'll grow rich in awareness of how complex life can be and realize the need that exists for writers who can help people connect to each other. You'll be famous in your own hometown as one of the few people with that special voice. (Unfortunately, perhaps, many will never know you were that voice, since greeting card writers rarely get their names put on their work. This varies with the publisher, though.) Is it worth the effort? I think so.

3 I KNOW THIS IS A GREAT IDEA!

Salable greeting card ideas require:

I nspiration
D evelopment
E valuation
A rt
S endability

Where do you get inspiration to write greeting cards? If you consider what a greeting card is—a card that "greets" or offers a friendly message to a specific person—you will find that inspiration is everywhere. Start with yourself and your interests. What hobbies do you have? What magazines do you read? What TV shows most capture your attention? What makes your day easy? Hard? Satisfying? What comic strip characters usually make you laugh? What kinds of situations do you find yourself in that you thought were funny? Sad? Silly? Embarrassing? Weird?

Two wonderful guys, Pete and Rick (known as the Kersten Brothers), have developed some fun characters for greeting cards. The card on the next page, from their "Sweet Corn" line reads, "It's not important to count birthdays. Just make them fun!" It's a great example of how art and copy enhance each other. Critter Tales, another favorite series from their lines, has incorporated a variety of seasons and everyday events. When asked what they think helps them create a new greeting card, the Kersten Brothers offered this thought.

Happy Birthday

We have found that there are two ways to create a greeting card: One, the writing inspires the visual, or two, the visual inspires the writing. That determination focuses our approach.

I am often asked, "Which comes first, the words or the art?" and this is a good chance to reflect along with the Kerstens that either can come first. The writing may inspire a variety of thoughts or images, or a particular image may inspire the right words. I believe that the more visual a writer is, the more success she will find in this business. A greeting card seeks to appeal to the consumer with both the art and the copy. Good writers always appreciate a visual that enhances the words.

31

How Can You Get Started?

You're surrounded with inspiration and you haven't yet set a pen to paper or your fingers to a keyboard. Let's choose hobbies as an example of where to get inspiration. One of my hobbies is reading. How can that help me with greeting card writing? I'll start with the books I have around the house. I have a particular interest in children's books, so I have quite a few of those. Dr. Seuss is a good start. *Oh, the Places You'll Go!* Reading through this magnificent book, I'm reminded that people are constantly facing change, new challenges, new beginnings and moments of confusion and loneliness. Right away, I have a wealth of greeting card possibilities. I can do some graduation cards about seeking new opportunities, or I can write retirement cards about facing the challenges that a retired life brings. I can simply write encouragement cards for those seeking new direction in new surroundings.

Let's look at the bookshelf again and see what else might inspire us. I have a book called *Meditations for Women Who Do Too Much*. Without even going through the book chapters, I can think about the many things so many women try to do today to keep up with homes, families, work, love and spiritual lives, community service and politics, and the wheels are spinning again. Now I can write cards for moms, sisters and friends that express appreciation, amazement, encouragement or in some humorous way, poke fun at how much one woman does in a day. It's a feast of greeting card possibilities.

I see books on friendships, romance, raising children, cooking, religion . . . all there waiting for me to discover what they might say if some form of their message were turned into a greeting card.

While we're still at home, what else might inspire us? What about *your* day? What happened to you in the past twenty-four hours that could easily become a greeting card situation? Now might be a good time to start that greeting card journal or keep that idea file handy. *You* are your own best subject! Did you give comfort to a friend today? Did you give praise to a child for a job well done? Did you tell a spouse "I love you"? Did you listen to a news broadcast about a woman on the verge of delivering eight babies? Were you awed? If you did any of those things, you're ready to write a greeting card. You're inspired!

Should I Watch More TV?

If you rented a movie or watched a TV program, you're also inspired. Think about what the movie was about or what the theme of the show was. What did you learn about relationships? Can you turn your favorite game show into a greeting card idea? Can you use talk shows or a home shopping channel as fuel for a great idea? Can you watch a political debate or *Sesame Street* and visualize a greeting card situation? Does *I Love Lucy* strike your funny bone so well you can find a way to make squashing grapes with your feet seem like fun in a greeting card? Does Mr. Rogers make you want to spell *birthday*, boys and girls? Did you see a moving episode of *ER* and relate more closely to someone in a traumatic life situation? Your day is always rich with ideas.

Can I Dream Up an Idea?

Disney's *Cinderella* thought a "dream is a wish your heart makes." Well, what's going on in your dreams? You might find some fascinating things from your dreams that inspire a new form of expression. Perhaps your dreams, thoughts and wishes will provide energy and inspiration for greeting cards. Do you seek a certain goal? Then you know what that feels like, and you can encourage someone else who may be working toward a goal, a college degree or a new house. Do you fantasize about the ideal relationship? Then you have more than enough fuel to weave a picture of beautiful romance and cast a spell on the heart of a loved one. Greeting cards are vehicles for dreams, and senders and recipients alike always hope they will come true.

Well, we've just hit the tip of the idea iceberg. You haven't left home and you've already generated a considerable number of potential ideas. Before we go shopping, let's look outside. What do you see? Is it raining today? Is there a rainbow? (There always is in greeting card land, you know.) Is the sun shining? Is the azalea bush in full bloom? Are the birds singing? Is a big, noisy truck cranking its gears outside your window? Is the street alive with people and dogs and traffic? Is it quiet and breezy and empty? Stopping to notice what is going on around you can give you a variety of places to begin a new greeting card verse. Looking more generally to the outdoors, nature and the world that surrounds you also offers you an opportunity for greeting card sales. Gardening cards are an industry staple. Floral quotations are used hundreds of times on a variety of products. All the symbolism that growth, horizons and clouds can bring has been classic material for inspiring greeting card sentiments.

Still outside with me? OK, what else is out there? Who's out there? A law enforcement officer walking the beat and a postal worker carrying a bag of mail? Should there be greeting cards for people in specific occupations? Should there be a line for the guy who cuts your meat, the woman who sells you flowers, and the manager at your favorite supermarket? Maybe. Maybe this is your ticket to inspiring a whole new promotion that a publisher will be glad to market.

Did you see anyone else on our walk? I did. I saw the elderly couple down the street who always have a kind word for everyone and who make strangers feel like friends almost instantly. I saw the young woman with two little toddlers trying to create a happy outing. I saw the teenagers on the corner who are wondering what it really means to be a kid and what it really means to be an adult. I saw the school where children are struggling to become educated enough to find a place in a world that may have changed right under their noses before they ever reach graduation day. All of these are inspiring. These are the things that make up the heart and soul of people's lives. Your job as a greeting card writer is to connect those souls and those hearts together and help them communicate a little more clearly, more deeply and perhaps a little more lovingly with each other. Your job is to be an unseen but universal voice, a missionary in the arena of human communication.

You can see Ziggy on the next page helping to keep the lines of communication open and connecting with a simple "hello." Sometimes that thought alone can reach into the heart of a person's day.

How Do You Develop Those Good Ideas?

You've gotten a bit of inspiration from home and from your neighborhood, so let's move on to the shopping mall. Greeting card writ-

Reprinted by permission of Ziggy & Friends, Inc. © 1996 Ziggy & Friends, Inc. Ziggy ® by Tom Wilson. Distributed by Universal Press Syndicate.

ers collect ideas from all kinds of stores. Bookstores offer an enormous array of subjects at various age levels. The titles of business books, for example, give me ideas for office co-worker, boss or other work-related cards. The appearance of *Dilbert* shows how much there is to mock in our corporate lives. The religious section gives me ideas about current topics for that market. It's important for you to know how to slant your work for a particular market

35

segment. You may find it a valuable use of your time to browse through Christian bookstores, New Age bookstores and others that offer specialty products. It's helpful for you to think about all the different types of customers that publishers are addressing. Those customers are your customers.

Of course, you'll want to visit independent greeting card and gift shops to see what's on the market. You need to know what's already out there so you can understand what works and so you won't duplicate what is there. Make sure you check out new stores when you're traveling. Different sections of the country offer different product looks and ideas.

Grocery stores and card stores aim at different buyers, so you'll want to see them all when you're comparing card racks. Craft stores offer a variety of products that may provide copy and packaging ideas. The Warner Brothers Stores and the Disney Stores are excellent resources for ideas that appeal to kids and grown-ups.

Take advantage of local art or history museums that can give you a better sense of a time period or a particular group of people. If you're attempting to write juvenile cards, you might find it helpful to visit toy stores, children's museums or even schools for inspiration. Talking to kids can be some of the best inspiration, especially if you tune in to what's important to them. And don't forget music stores and video stores for trends and current topics.

Have a game plan when you go reference shopping because you will be more productive. Try to focus on a specific market area when you go to search. If you want to write humor, then shop for humorous cards only. If you're into sentimental cards, read those. Pay attention to things like artwork, verse style, what information you get about the relationship and level of emotion being expressed. Was the card written in a rhyme or with a simple wish in a conversational tone? Was the card one that you would send? Could you spin an idea in a new direction based on a card that you read? Could you see a way to expand an idea into a whole series of cards? Did you look on the back of the card to see if the design or the copy continued there? Be sure to take a notebook with you so you can jot down leads and ideas as they occur to you.

Cathy Guisewite, the celebrated creator of *Cathy*, passed along the following thought about what makes a good greeting card. "My best test for a greeting card is always whether or not I'd send it to anyone myself." Her advice is well taken. If you wouldn't buy the card you wrote, don't submit it to a publisher. You have to like your work when you're writing greeting cards.

A contract writer for Gibson Greetings offered this little tip.

> When I buy cards I admire, I make a copy for my own greeting card idea file before sending the card. I also file copies of great cards I receive. It certainly has built up a helpful file over the years.

How Do You Decide if Your Idea Is Strong?

How many people could buy your idea? How universal is it in its appeal in terms of art and copy? The salability of an idea is determined by looking at its limitations. The limitations come from many directions.

- Are the words too lofty or too juvenile? Do they talk down to the reader or appear to be patronizing?
- Is the word *I* in the verse? Cards that must be either single senders or multiple senders have built-in limitations.
- Is the main topic of the verse a limitation? Does it talk about growing up with someone or having a child?
- Is the wording so effusive that the sender and receiver must have a strong, intimate relationship for the card to be purchased?
- The most salable cards are those that can be purchased by the most consumers, such as: "Happy Birthday," "Thinking of You," "Wishing You Life's Good Things." Salable, but limiting: "I Love You!"
- Test out your sentiment on a few others before you send it. Ask them to rate your piece on a scale of one to five. Only send the ones you all agree are fives.

What About Writing to Art?

Writing to art means writing your copy to accompany a certain piece or style of art. You don't need to know the names of famous artists or all the techniques that might be used on a greeting card, but having a feel for the art is certainly a benefit to you as a writer. On one of your card shopping excursions, take some time and just concentrate on the art. Without reading the verse on the card, try to imagine what you would have written for that art. Then read the card and see if you were anywhere close to what was published. Greeting card publishers work hard to put the right art and copy combinations together. Even the lettering style should enhance the card and help to carry the tone or the mood of the message more accurately.

Another way you can practice writing to art is to find as many nouns as you can and write them down from a piece of greeting card art. Let's say you have a fall scene of a winding road and a small house with puffs of smoke coming from the chimney. Imagine this is a Father's Day card and you have to describe feelings about growing up with Dad. You can start by listing some of those images on the card and then begin a verse using your word list. This will also help you to begin to pay attention to all the details of a greeting card.

Do you have to send in artwork with your greeting card idea? No, not usually. Sometimes you can help the editor understand your idea better if you do send a little sketch, but it certainly isn't necessary.

The drawing on the following page is an example of the way one writer submits art suggestions with his copy. This writer likes to visually represent his copy idea. He has an art background; however, many writers do not. That shouldn't stop you from submitting ideas. You can always describe the artwork in words. Think about this visual of the cat catching buckets of mice and decide what copy you would write for it. This writer offered several copy directions on small sticky notes when he submitted it.

Sometimes these sketches are used to help develop the actual art on the card, or they help to illustrate the idea to editor and, therefore, get it purchased.

Eva Szela's book *The Complete Guide to Greeting Card Design & Illustration* is an excellent resource for artistic approaches commonly used in the greeting card industry. You'll learn subject matter and the techniques that work, but you'll also have a guide to the

sending situations that you need to write to. It can be helpful to review a book like this, look at the art and the copy that was used and then, using the same art, come up with new copy. You'll discover that several styles of writing will carry the right tone for the art and create a special message for the recipient. You can also do this exercise with old cards or magazine photos you have around the house. Though a large portion of greeting card writing is done first, before the art is generated, it is sometimes necessary to be able to write to a particular design.

Still Looking for Inspiration?
Ah, inspiration! It's in the newspaper and in the waiting room of the hospital. It's in the restaurant guide of the city magazine and in

the yellow pages. It's in the local news on TV and the radio station that wakes you up each morning. It's in the store where you shopped today and the place where you got your hair cut. It's in the conversation you had with your four-year-old and in the phone chat you had with your grandmother. It's in cyberspace at a thousand different Web sites. As you learn to be an observer of life, you'll find that you have more to write about. Your portfolio of ideas widens with every relationship you share.

 IDEA JOGGER

Take one basic idea and change it four times so that you increase the depth of the relationship with each sentiment. Begin with the wish "Happy Birthday!" That's number one. Now, keep adding to the sentiment and create three more sentiments that express more relationship depth with each verse.

Here's an example: 1. *Happy Birthday.* 2. *Wishing you a joyful birthday.* 3. *You deserve the best birthday ever.* 4. *You're so important to me, I can't help hoping that your birthday will be the beginning of a wonderful year of happiness.*

You can see that each step showed a deeper connection between the recipient and the sender. Your job as a writer is to help create that positive connection between senders and recipients. How you express that depth and that relationship connection can happen in a variety of ways. Let's keep looking at how to grow an idea.

Let's focus on the religious market to demonstrate the variety of ways you can meet special needs there. Let's say you've been to a Christian bookstore and discovered that specific terminology is used by some publishers. You noted key phrases like "praying for you," "seeking a miracle on your behalf" or "believing in God's promises to help you with your personal concerns." Now, what can you do with this information to create a meaningful greeting card?

IDEA 1: PRAYING FOR YOU
You can go the direct and most obvious route:

> *Just want you to know*
> *I'm praying for you today.*

You can be less direct:

> *You're always in my thoughts*
> *and in my prayers.*

You can even be more direct:

> *I talked to God about you today. . . .*

IDEA 2: SEEKING A MIRACLE ON YOUR BEHALF
Most obvious:

> *I've been thinking about you*
> *and asking God for a miracle to heal you.*

Less direct:

> *I sent up a prayer for you*
> *and am trusting God for your healing.*

More direct:

> *I don't know if you believe in miracles,*
> *but I do, and I'm asking God to grant a miracle*
> *in your life.*

IDEA 3: BELIEVING IN GOD'S PROMISES TO HELP YOU
WITH YOUR PERSONAL CONCERNS
Direct: You can use a Bible quotation and then complete it. For
example, 1 Peter 5:7 (NIV) says:

Cast all your anxiety on him because he cares for you.
I hope you know that I'm here for you, 'cause I care,
too.

Another approach:

*I know you've been going through some difficult times
and I want you to know that I've been praying for you
and trusting God to take care of all your needs.*

Now, let's get a more detailed understanding of conventional
writing styles.

What Writing Styles Are Preferred?

Editors are looking for a variety of styles, but one thing you should
note is the difference between writing poetry and writing greeting
card sentiments. I received this thought from Holly Davis, Writing
Manager at Gibson Greetings. "Nothing brands a greeting card
writer as an amateur as much as calling up and saying he wants to
submit his *poems.*" Greeting card editors do not consider greeting
card editorial as poetry. What is the difference? In poetry, the author takes on words to express his or her own thoughts or feelings.
In greeting cards, the author lends words to thousands of others to
express their thoughts and feelings. Superlatives, ideals and specific
detail do not work well with greeting cards because they may not
be true to the sender's or recipient's specific needs or experiences.
Also, tricks of language encouraged in poetry are often avoided in
greeting cards because these forms of expression do not generally
feel natural to the sender.

Make sure you understand this difference between poetry and
greeting card sentiments before you submit ideas. As the manager of
the editorial department at Current, Inc., I can tell you that we often
receive batches of poetry. Since it is rare for us to be able to use poems,
we generally just send them back to the freelancer. Greeting card editors are looking for me-to-you sentiments for their lines.

Though you may find more options are available to you if you
can write off-the-wall, edgy humor, that's not all there is. Conven-

tional writing is strongly needed and is still the cornerstone of birthday, anniversary, wedding and get well lines, and major seasons like Christmas and Valentine's Day. Nearly every card category offers a few conventional cards, even if the words are only "Thank You" or "Thinking of You Today."

Deciding What to Say

How do you decide what to say in a conventional verse? First, you check the writer's guidelines from the publisher, or you check the listing in the latest *Writer's Market* to get a good sense of what publishers are looking for. The following tips were all taken from recent listings:

- "Happy Birthday" sells the best.
- Tie into current trends.
- Make sure your writing keeps up with the times.
- Give your ideas a personal touch. Have someone in mind when you write.
- Unrhymed verse is preferred.
- Looking for short, inspirational verse, rhymed or not, upbeat, with an emotional jolt of familiar feeling.
- Sentiments conversational in tone and format preferred.
- Communicate situations, thoughts and relationships in a new or fun way.
- The best cards have mass appeal and yet, in the consumer's eyes, will read as though they were created exclusively for her. A feminine touch is important as 90 percent of all greeting cards are purchased by women.
- Make sentiments sendable, personal and positive.
- Religious themes work for us.

The best advice about conventional writing is to write from the heart and say something meaningful. Most publishers have simple wishes and compliments in their lines. They need contemporary views on what relationships are all about. We usually categorize the messages by what the most limiting theme of the card is. When you write a phrase like "I love you," you can see that the word *love* limits the number of people you can send that card to. Therefore, when you write, keep the theme of the card in mind.

Carl Goeller divided conventional themes into formulas in his book *Writing and Selling Greeting Cards*. One formula offers a sentiment that begins with a statement or a belief. "It's your birthday and I was thinking of you. . . ." Another formula begins the sentiment with a problem. "Since I can't be with you on your birthday. . . ." Sometimes the problem is exaggerated and becomes improbable. Today's publishers are getting away from some formulas in conventional writing because they prefer more realistic and honest situations. They want to look at life situations in positive and *real* ways. Juvenile cards are still a good place to use formulas, however, so don't throw them out entirely. "If Big Bird could visit you today" might be the beginning of an improbable, but still fun formula approach. Imagination is the key to good juvenile writing.

Another convention is to begin the card with a flattering remark or a compliment. "Nobody brightens my life like you do!" When you write, try to have someone in mind and imagine that you are really speaking to her person-to-person, heart-to-heart. Read your piece to someone and see if it is received with the intention you had when you wrote it. Make sure all the connections were made so that it flows easily from one idea to another. Here's an example of a well-written conventional verse.

FOR YOUR BIRTHDAY . . .
What would you enjoy the most—
A party to attend?
Being with your family?
Chatting with a friend?
Dreaming of that special day
You find the rainbow's end?
Hope that's what your birthday brings to you!

What about some time to do
Exactly as you please,
From looking for excitement
To just sitting back at ease . . .
Or feeling good as you recall
Some treasured memories?
Hope that's what your birthday brings to you!

Whatever makes you happy
And whatever sounds like fun,
Whatever fills your day with smiles
To share with everyone,
Whatever puts the magic
In each minute till it's done,
Hope that's what your birthday brings to you!

This contemporary, conversational rhyme was written by Nancy Breen, an in-house writer for Gibson Greetings. I asked Nancy to give you a few more tips to help you in your writing adventures.

I agree that pretending you're actually talking or writing to the recipient of a card is the best way to make it sound conversational and contemporary. Even if the verse is in rhyme, a direct, one-to-one communication style counteracts the tendency to be too formal. There's something about rhyme, whether it's card verses or poetry, that makes writers think they have to put on a pose and become stilted. This just produces starchy, dull verses.

It actually can be helpful to brainstorm in this more casual, conversational mode. For instance, say you are writing a birthday wish card. Begin with a straightforward "I'm wishing you . . ." and then write statement after statement of everything you might wish for that person. It could be the typical "I'm wishing you blue skies and sunshine" to "I'm wishing you unending cake and a bottomless tub of ice cream!" Don't self-edit, just let the words flow. Not only is this good training for conversational writing, but it also gives you an invaluable store of raw material from which to draw for all kinds of cards. Try this exercise for other situations. "I'm glad we're friends because . . ." or "Thank you for . . ." or "I love it when . . ." or anything else that's appropriate.

Read lots of good contemporary card verses and poetry! There are plenty of accessible, enjoyable poems out there, both prose and rhyme, that have many of the same qualities as good card writing: tightness, naturally flowing rhythm, a direct conversational style. If you have the opportunity to hear poets read their work, whether recorded, broadcast or live, do so. Even poorly performed work will teach you something about the difference between spoken lines and lines that are frozen on the page. When you read your poems aloud, pretend you're actually reading/saying them to someone in the room. This really helps your ear to hear the proper rhythm of solid, down-to-earth writing.

Sometimes you'll be asked to write for a very specific occasion or recipient. Here's an example by former Gibson editor Tricia Thelen from a Mother's Day line that addresses the single mother.

> *You should be very pleased*
> *with your accomplishments.*
> *After all, being a parent*
> *takes a lot of time,*
> *and doing it alone*
> *is especially hard.*
> *So as you continue to care and love*
> *and hold your family in your heart,*
> *remember that you're special*
> *and what you're doing*
> *is something to be proud of.*

Conversational Prose

As you can see, this last sentiment offers a more direct and honest assessment of what a single mother situation may be like. Blue Mountain Arts built its reputation on just such conversational prose and even the big companies try to emulate them. Hallmark's "Between You and Me" line is also a good example of personal, conversational prose. Consumers like meaningful prose, so focus on your feelings for someone and begin to write. I suggest that before you write this type of conventional copy, you go out and read some good prose lines in the racks. Hallmark recently featured some of their writers in a line called "New Voices." This is quite a unique step for the industry, since real writers are not often the focus of a card line. The varied conventional approaches offered in this line are both contemporary and real.

Tips From the Pros

The following are tips I've received from other industry professionals about writing for conventional, religious or juvenile markets. I'll cover humorous markets in another chapter.

But First, a Couple (OK, Five) More Thoughts From Me . . .

1. Never throw away those wonderful product catalogs offering everything from clothes to windsocks to housewares (at least not before you've gleaned some good leads from them). I especially enjoy ones like *Seasons, Cold Water Creek, Red Rose* and *Wireless.* Here are some examples of lead lines that were taken from catalogs that work well for greeting card writing.

- May we treat one another with respect, honesty and care. . . .
- May we share the little discoveries and changes each day brings. . . .
- I can't imagine in all the world a better friend than you. . . .

2. Magazine ads offer hundreds of situations for writing new card sentiments. Recently, I was working on a promotion (a special group of cards sold together) that was built around a theme of coffee/tea images. I was surprised at how many ads I could find that offered words or images that helped to pull that card promotion together.

3. Consider all the formats that cards can take, such as photo insert cards or cards with tiny cards or little gift books added. These can be a nice touch to an assortment idea that you could sell a publisher. The Hallmark Gold Crown lines have been trying a wide variety of attachments on cards. Looking through these should help you discover other ideas for attachments.

4. Remember that as baby boomers get older, there will be a greater need for grandchildren and grandparent cards. Can you come up with new ideas for those markets? I read one statistic that

stated ten thousand people turn fifty every day. That means that there will be a gigantic number of grandparents in the world in the next few years. The Senior market is going to continue to move many industries, as seniors will be the people with the largest amount of disposable income. You've probably noticed that the focus of advertising is no longer just on the very young. We now celebrate age as well. I also read an article about the reluctance of manufacturers and marketing people to keep up with the growing demands of the baby boomer seniors. The greeting card industry will have to get behind this trend to stay successful in the next millennium because this group has the most power and influence.

5. Remember when you write for seniors that you're spanning an age range of grandparents anywhere from forty to one hundred years old. We need to address their lifestyles and needs in a variety of ways. We've tended to keep this group safely tucked under the florals and violets and depicted all our grandmas as sweet little ladies with rocking chairs and their hair in a bun. Those days are gone. Today's grandmas are active, often working full-time jobs, exercising, and in general keeping much more fit than any generation before them. Write to those people. Imagine Cher and Goldie Hawn and Tina Turner as grandmas because that's the age group we're addressing. It's time for a whole new image in those card racks.

Advice From the Experts

First, here's Debbie Paul from American Greetings.

> Study cards produced by different greeting card companies before writing your own. Really get to know the market. Don't just assume that you know what makes a good greeting card already. Keep in mind that our greeting card company has over 100,000 sentiments in our computer bank, so more often than not, material sent in for review by freelancers is returned with the comment "we already have similar." Just as originality in art style is important to the visual arts, so is orginality in phrasing a message for a greeting card. After all, writing is an art,

4 IF A ROSE IS A ROSE, SHOULD IT BE RHYME OR PROSE?

Let's look at the ways to determine what form your writing should take. Greeting cards once had a reputation for offering singsongy rhyme that carried a beat and set your head a-nodding to the rhythm so much that you almost didn't think about the meaning of the words themselves. Rhyme is still very important for occasions like birthday, anniversary and Christmas. In fact, even today, long rhyme outsells other writing styles. So why is it harder to sell rhyme to a greeting card publisher? Publishers bank—that is, keep in storage—the material they have used or plan to use in the near future. That means their files are full of sentiments that sell well for them. It doesn't mean they've got every good rhyme possible, though. Let's see if we can cut through the mysterious, beyond all the serious and find the delirious path to your sales. (OK, *you* try to rhyme a word with *mysterious* and *serious*).

Good Rhyme

First, if you need a good refresher course on writing rhymed verse in general, I suggest you get a good rhyming dictionary and play with some of the rhyme patterns that you see there. A little time spent running, punning and funning through the pages should give you a good start. If you need some basic poetic building devices, I recommend *How to Write & Sell Greeting Cards, Bumper Stickers, T-Shirts and Other Fun Stuff* by Molly Wigand or a good beginning poetry book like Jeff Mock's *You Can Write Poetry.*

I assume that you already have a pretty good sense of whether you write pieces that might be salable. (If you don't, keep reading the examples given throughout this book and then try some of the suggestions in the workbook section at the end.) Here are some thoughts on rhyme that you might want to consider.

1. A good greeting card rhyme should always have a clear message. The person who receives your rhyme should have a good sense of the main ideas and the intent of the verse. One mistake poets make in submitting rhyme is that they forget the need for a clear me-to-you message. Sending in a beautiful love poem that you wrote after being zinged by a flood of Cupid's arrows may work, but only if it isn't too personal. Remember, your idea has to work for thousands of senders and receivers.

2. Sometimes freelancers are not aware that their rhymes must have a consistent meter (that is the number of beats in a line—the rhythm section). It's OK for meter to be irregular if it reads well, but it can't be too far off. Greeting card writers and editors throughout the industry probably all disagree on this point. Some won't accept anything but perfect meter (perfect to their ear, that is), and some won't accept near rhyme (affair and shares), and others look for patterns that they like best. You may have learned about iambic pentameter, but rhyme patterns are nearly endless, and a good writer will try all kinds of interesting ones to give freshness and new life to a sentiment. Do avoid the *oo-you, ay-day* rhyme patterns if you can because they've been done over and over again. Try other devices like internal rhyme and unrhymed last lines and even sonnets and villanelles to strengthen your rhyme life. A good dose of Ogden Nash, Shel Silverstein, Dr. Seuss and Robert Frost and you'll start to get the idea of rhyme patterns.

3. The next thing to keep in mind is the actual content of your message. You not only want it to rhyme, but in today's market you want the rhyme to take a backseat to the message itself. I think this

is the strongest difference in the way we value rhymed verse today over past years. You really want to say something personal and meaningful and worthwhile. Good rhyme can and should have the emotional impact of solid prose (unrhymed verse). Your message should make the reader *feel* what you have to say. It should cause a response—laughter, tears, joy, wistfulness—some heartfelt and real emotion. So, take a look at that piece you want to submit, give it to someone who hasn't read it before and see how he responds (not your best friend, of course, unless you think he'll really give you an honest response).

4. Another thing you can do when you write rhyme is to read it aloud. When you do that, you can usually hear whether it has the right rhythm. If you play an instrument, you may indeed have a better sense of rhythm, but it's not really necessary for writing salable rhymed verse. Here's a contemporary rhyme from Nancy Breen.

> *Birthday happiness can be served up*
> *in many delightful ways. . . . (this part is the lead-in)*

> *So many ways to celebrate a birthday,*
> *so many happy choices you can make—*
> *an evening out, some time alone, a party,*
> *a quiet conversation over cake.*
> *Whatever kind of birthday suits your fancy,*
> *don't waste a single moment—have a ball!*
> *Hope everything about your celebration*
> *brings lots of special moments to recall.*
> *Happy Birthday*

You can see that this rhyme makes some real suggestions about how the birthday could be celebrated and then adds a warm wish.

Advice About Rhyme

In checking with the experts on other advice about writing rhymed verse, I received these tips from Debbie Paul, senior editor for American Greetings.

Don't assume that poetry is greeting card material. Greeting card verse has a me-to-you message and is written to be used by hundreds of people. Write what you believe others would like to say directly to someone they care about.

Also, when you write a rhymed sentiment, make it sound so conversational that it can be read like prose. This is not easy to do, but it's very important. Your message must sound personal and as casual as a written note. You should avoid any words that force a rhyme or cause you to manipulate words simply for the sake of the rhyme.

We treat humorous rhyme a bit differently, and we'll consider that in more detail in chapter six. Some of these observations still apply there, but additional formats are utilized.

Examples of Good Rhyme
Before we leave this section on rhyme, let me give you a few more good examples.

Strong imagery:

> *Have a pink cotton candy and grape lollipop,*
> *sundae with nuts (and a cherry) on top,*
> *Gummy bear, caramel, licorice whip,*
> *oven-fresh cookie and big chocolate chip,*
> *Soda-pop float, toasted marshmallow treat,*
> *warm peanut brittle and butterscotch sweet,*
> *Popcorn ball, taffy and tart lemon drop*
> *kind of day that's delicious from start until stop!*

Unrhymed last line:

> *Aphids on roses*
>   *and mildew on asters,*
> *Leaks in the hoses*
>   *and lawn grub disasters,*
> *Droughts in the summers*
>   *and floods in the springs,*

These are a few
of my least favorite things. . . .
Hope your birthday
brings only your favorite ones!

Here are a few different rhyme scheme patterns that will be good for you to use as models for writing practice:

Trees are budding!
Birds are singing!
Grass is growing!
Spring is springing!
Flowers are blooming!
Bees are humming!
Obviously, Easter's coming!

Have a Happy Easter!

You can see in this rhyme that there is no me-to-you message in the verse itself. That part is handled with a tag wish. This is sometimes an acceptable format.

This one uses a repetition of the phrase "we share."

We share a special family
And a home that we both love,
We share the same warm memories
And things we're dreaming of,
We share the ups and downs of life
As seasons come and go . . .
And I treasure all the things we share
Because I love you so.

Here's another example utilizing a repeated phrase.

Whatever it is
that would please you the most,
whatever you're hoping will be,

Whatever you'd like
to spend your time doing,
whatever you'd most like to see . . .
Whatever it is
that would make you feel special,
happy and lighthearted too—
Well, that's what this wishes,
and wishes with love,
because it's especially for you.

These two use a refrain line technique.

I'm thinking of you
'cause it's Easter,
I'm thinking of you
'cause it's spring,
I'm thinking of you
'cause I like all the smiles
That thinking of you
always brings!

And . . .

Few things can match the feeling
of love and joy and pride
That a dear and special daughter
can bring, deep down inside. . . .
Few things can match the happiness
the warmth and caring, too,
That are such a part of having
a daughter just like you!

 IDEA
JOGGER

Study this little rhyme chart, then use it to create sentiments for
kids.

Toot, suit, route, jute, flute, lute, newt, pollute, cute, pursuit, fruit, moot, hoot

Cherry, berry, carry, wary, scary, fairy, sherry, query, airy, beary, hairy, marry

Attack, Jack, smack, shack, lack, tack, stack, whack, crack, knack, black, back, sack

Glare, dare, affair, share, rare, wear, prayer, fair, mare, dare, hare, stair, chair, air

Touché, hooray, today, away, astray, Mayday, payday, OK, olé, betray, heyday

Tricks, kicks, sticks, pricks, wicks, flicks, bricks, clicks, fix, mix, six, ticks, schticks

Plop, flop, stop, shop, drop, cop, whop, slop, mop, chop, clop, hop, glop, bebop

Clock, stock, rock, shock, squawk, walk, jock, knock, flock, block, dock, mock

Dough, grow, throw, go, show, flow, below, know, yo-yo, tow, aglow, gallow, woe

Try new rhyme patterns! ABCB (the first and third lines don't rhyme, but the second and fourth *do*) is a nice one. AAB, AAB is another. Pretend you're Shel Silverstein or e.e. cummings and just have fun with pattern and rhyme. You'll find your writing will open up and present many new possibilities. Publishers will welcome your efforts because these fresh ideas bring new life to the core lines. Try writing a romantic sonnet for Valentine's Day.

Prose

OK, let's take a closer look at prose writing styles and what you can do with them.

The greeting card industry has long debated the appeal of rhyme over prose writing and vice versa. The pendulum swings one direction and then the other. Obviously, consumers find something valuable in both kinds of verse writing because both sell well. Christmas box cards, formal cards and sympathy cards typically work better with prose styles. A good prose sentiment needs to have the charm of a rhymed verse but be more direct and personal in its approach to the reader. Your prose should come from the heart.

Whether your prose piece is five words or fifty words, you need to make sure that each word has a purpose, just as in rhyme. If a word is only there as a filler, meaning it isn't adding anything to the clarity or development of the idea, then take it out. It's pretty easy with prose to find yourself rambling and, before you know it, creating a lifeless piece. Greeting card writers use a number of techniques to help them develop prose styles.

The devices most often used have to do with alliteration or the structure of the lines. Even in prose, structure is important. Let's look at a few examples.

Alliteration

Alliteration refers to the repetition of certain beginning sounds in a given piece of writing. Some of the best examples can be found in the tongue twisters we all grew up with.

> She sells seashells by the seashore!

> If Peter Piper picked a peck of pickled peppers, where's the peck of pickled peppers Peter Piper picked?

Of course, we don't apply this device quite this strictly in most greeting card verses (unless we choose to for humor or juvenile cards), but we do use it to structure prose. In a sentiment, we might write:

> *May the magic of Christmas,*
> *make your heart merry*
> *with moments*
> *of laughter and love.*

You can see the repetition of the letter *m* and of the *l* in the last line. Another form of structured prose happens when we repeat a certain line throughout the piece as in this next example:

Structured Prose

> *Where you are,*
> *there are tender arms,*
> *a welcoming smile,*
> *a scent of perfume in the air . . .*
> *Where you are,*
> *there are bright dreams to share,*
> *lots of laughter, warmhearted teasing,*
> *caring and helping . . .*
> *Where you are,*
> *there is love.*

You can see in this form that the prose is very much like rhymed poetry. It has a definite feeling of rhythm.

Another way to strengthen your prose writing is to take rhymed verses and rewrite them in prose formats. Let's take an example:

> *Forever is too short a time*
> *For me to share with you,*
> *Together, as we dream our dreams*
> *And watch them coming true. . . .*
> *And always isn't long enough*
> *To show my love, I know,*
> *For, with the passing of the years,*
> *That love can only grow. . . .*
> *A lifetime is too little time,*
> *And all eternity*
> *Can't hold the happiness I've found*
> *When you are close to me.*

OK, let's rewrite this one in prose form.

> *Forever is too short a time for us to*
> *share our dreams and watch them come true.*
> *Always isn't enough time either, because I know*
> *that through the years our love for each other*

will just keep growing.
I don't even think a lifetime or all eternity
would be enough time to share all the happiness
I've found just having you close to me.

Though we've maintained the structure—in this case, a time comparison throughout the piece—we can see that the prose piece offers a different mood to the reader than the rhyme. Rewriting rhymed verse into prose and taking prose pieces and changing them into metered rhyme are excellent ways to develop your own writing style.

Other Prose Approaches

Another approach is to take literary quotes and write a companion piece that either expands or enhances them in some way. Here are a couple examples.

What is life?
It is the flash of a firefly in the night.
It is the breath of a buffalo in the winter time.
It is the little shadow which runs across the grass
and loses itself in the Sunset.
—Crowfoot
Your companion piece may go something like this:

What is life?
It is the joy I feel whenever you're near.
It is the melody in your laughter
and the music in your smile.
It is the glow of love that fills my heart
day after day, because the best part of my life
is you.

Or, it might be something simpler, like:

May your birthday be
a true celebration of life.

Another quote:

> *Consider the grasses and the oaks,*
> *the swallows, the sweet butterfly—*
> *they are one and all*
> *a sign and token*
> *showing before our eyes*
> *earth made into life.*
> —*Richard Jeffries*

A companion piece might be:

> *Celebrating the day you were born.*

Or:

> *When I think of all the things on earth*
> *that give it beauty*
> *and bring it to life,*
> *I can't help thinking of you*
> *and all the beauty*
> *you bring to my life.*
> *Thank you.*

Fresh Language, Fresh Ideas

It's sometimes difficult in greeting card writing, especially in prose, to resist falling into timeworn clichés. In conventional prose, that might include things like "wishing you sunshine and rainbows," "hearts and flowers," or even "pansies stand for thoughts." It's all right to start there when you're practicing, but try to discover fresher ways to deliver your messages. A good cliché book will remind you what to avoid—or in writing humor, give you leads. Metaphors are still practical devices for greeting card writing because whether in prose or rhyme, creating an image in words is important. If you need a reminder about the differences between metaphor and simile, here's a definition. Metaphor usually makes a comparison between two separate objects by saying that one thing IS something else: The sun *is* a golden medallion hanging in the sky. Simile

61

employs the same device but says that one thing is LIKE another: The sun is *like* a golden medallion hanging in the sky. These devices are important to greeting card writers when employed effectively.

Go to a local card retailer and jot down a few lead lines from some of the cards you see, either rhyme or prose, and then try to develop them in new ways. Try some of the following:

> *When I think of you . . .*
> *Being apart makes me realize . . .*
> *Please remember . . .*
> *You filled my life with . . .*
> *I love you because . . .*
> *What's really important to me is . . .*
> *You're a special friend because . . .*
> *I wonder if you understand . . .*
> *Don't ever doubt that I . . .*
> *I always knew that you'd succeed because . . .*
> *Thanks for helping me to . . .*
> *You're a source of joy to me . . .*
> *Morning, noon, and night, I (love you, miss you, think of*
>   *you, etc.) . . .*
> *Love is . . .*
> *Happiness is . . .*
> *Marriage is . . .*
> *Graduation is . . .*
> *A birthday is . . .*
> *A sister is . . .*

Phrases like these are some of the essential ingredients of greeting card writing. The best thing that you can do is read, read, read from local greeting card racks and then write, write, write until you move beyond the clichés and begin to develop contemporary, fresh and exciting approaches that will make publishers take notice. The feelings people need and want to express have not changed over the years. The ways we have elected to convey those feelings and the words we would choose have changed a great deal. Honesty, sincerity and authenticity play a much bigger role in social expression writing today. Think of how many cards you see on racks today that address issues like sympathy over losing your job or getting divorced, or wishing success to someone in a twelve-step recovery program. Honesty with compassion is much in demand in greeting card writing.

Consider the Consumer's Needs

Reading back through the pages of some of the former books on greeting card writing, I can see the changes that have taken place. Trends and current buzzwords in contemporary society make a difference in what is used in greeting cards today. It's important to know as much as you can about what's hot and what's not. You can be sure that publishers everywhere are paying attention to what's going on in the world.

One thing that greeting card companies often do is called segmentation research. What they most want to understand in this research is who their customers are and what their customers want. Whether they use focus groups, letters written by consumers to the company or mall intercept tests, they need to find out just what it is people are looking for. Let's look at some reasons why greeting cards are purchased today.

- moving from family and friends
- having more time and money
- getting married and increasing family size
- more family events—engagements, marriages, babies, graduations, deaths
- sending cards to kids in college or children with other parent
- less time than ever for letter writing
- old enough now to have greater appreciation of parents
- needing more get well and sympathy cards
- greeting cards offer greater selection than they used to (more sending situations)
- more people are in need of encouragement
- sending fewer Christmas cards, but more cards year-round
- consumers like to send funny cards to their friends for no special reason
- sometimes it's easier to send a greeting card to say something

than to try to say it in person
- some consumers see their card purchase as a gift
- a card is less expensive than a long-distance phone call
- some consumers consider their cards to be keepsakes
- cards can help to strengthen relationships

 IDEA JOGGER

Keeping in mind the reasons why consumers purchase cards should help as you face a blank screen. Use some of the reasons listed above and write a greeting card sentiment. What's it like to move far away from family and friends? How does it feel to be the one moving? How about the one left behind? How might a parent feel when a child first goes off to college? Happy? Sad? Worried? How can you address these feelings?

Picturesque Language

Another way to enhance your writing in prose or rhyme is to use very idealized images that will put the reader in a pleasant mood or convey the feelings of the card more clearly.

Some examples of images that have been used follow:
- *softly, tenderly, gently Christmas comes—not with the jingle of sleigh bells or the glitter of tinsel, but with quiet acts of kindness and caring words of love*
- *the One who can solve any problem, lift any burden, calm any storm is with you now*
- *like a cozy kitchen on a frosty day . . .*
- *from sunny skies to stormy weather . . .*
- *sunrise and rainbows*
- *stars proclaim the darkest night . . .*

- *keep a rainbow in your heart . . .*
- *happy home, beautiful memories, bright future . . .*
- *happiness is a butterfly . . .*
- *waking earth at springtime*
- *bright horizons filled with dreams*

 IDEA
JOGGER

What kinds of images do you feel strongly about? Can you create similes, metaphors and other beautiful descriptive forms for new greeting cards? Can you use some of the lead lines above to create your own sentiments?

5 IS THERE A DIFFERENCE BETWEEN BEING CUTE AND BEING CLEVER?

Before we head into the humor chapter, let's consider some lighter approaches that are used in many greeting card lines. Cute cards and clever cards are apples and oranges. They have a similar look but appeal to different tastes in buyers and have a different job to do.

Let's Be Cute

Cute cards are typically illustrated with sweeter art looks—baby animals, whimsical kittens, little girls in big bonnets. Something in the art and copy should turn your heart to mush. The copy on these is also cute and it may or may not try to match the art. Most often, the copy on cards like this could work with any number of cute art approaches. Cute cards are designed for a woman-to-woman audience of buyers who want to send wishes or thoughts, not always connected to an occasion, to someone they care about. Perhaps this example will give you an idea of what a cute card is meant to accomplish.

> *A little Easter*
> *keep-in-touch*
> *Because you're*
> *thought about*
> *so much!*

You can see that this is short, snappy copy that doesn't really discuss the relationship. Cute cards are almost like sending a smile or a bit of sunshine in an envelope. Here are a few more examples.
This prose goes with art depicting a droopy-eyed dog.

> *Without you . . .*
> *I've got the lonelies.*

Here's another prose example.

> *I thank my lucky stars . . .*
> *for you and the wonderful life*
> *we share.*

The rhyme in this verse is lilting, adding to the "cute" feeling.

> *A grateful note*
> *to tell you clearly,*
> *Your thoughtfulness*
> *is cherished dearly . . .*
> *Thank you warmly*
> *and sincerely!*

A cute getwell rhyme.

> *Someone like you*
> *is too nice to be sick . . .*

So couldn't you,
wouldn't you
feel better quick?

Cute verse is an industry staple and a style that you can develop fairly quickly. I've been told by experienced writers that it helps to immerse yourself in sugary thoughts or at least to read a number of these cards to help you get started. You may not be able to write them cold turkey, but if you break out the cookies and milk, you might do just fine. Cute cards are also used to bridge the gap between juvenile cards and the more grown-up variety. These often are just the right choice for preteen girls and sweet grandmas. Personally, I enjoy writing cute copy. It's a great way for an eternal optimist like me to escape from the real world. I think sweet, happy thoughts and, like Tinkerbell, wing my way into greeting card never-never land. If you want to go there, here are a few leads for you to try.

Passing by with a friendly "hi" . . .
Thinkin' 'boutcha . . .
Someone who's as sweet as you . . .
A bright bouquet of wishes . . .
Warmest thoughts and wishes . . .
Sunny thoughts . . .
Birthday candles shining bright . . .

Being Clever

Clever cards are closer to traditional humorous card lines and are usually mixed in with humor assortments. Unlike cute cards, clever ones usually tie in to the art very carefully. The marriage here is very important for the whole card to work. Clever cards are generally wordplays, simple parodies or puns that take a different twist on the art than you might have suspected when you first saw the card. The art is usually softer and sweeter than full-blown humor cards. Clever cards are for a wide range of recipients and are reliably safe to send to your grandmother. Let's look at a few examples.

This classic idea is accompanied by art of squirrels in a tree surrounded by acorns.

You belong in our family tree. . . .
It was a nutty one to begin with!

This birthday card is for boys and features race car artwork.

Racing in just to say . . .
When it comes to other birthday boys . . .
. . . you beat 'em by a mile!

All kinds of frog art could accompany this verse.

Hope you're hoppin' around again soon. . . .
Don't frog-et to take good care of yourself!

Picture a small cartoon bunny handing a bouquet of carrots to its grandmother.

Grandma, I love you a whole bunch!

 IDEA JOGGER

Clever is having a rich pun life, a fresh perspective on what a phrase could mean. Clever is taking words and playing with images that could marry them in silly or fun ways. Try some copy or design ideas with these words.

rubber band
sidewalk
jaywalk
workhorse
fur ball

flip side
put two and two together
get in over your head
get dolled up
make a clean sweep
make a monkey out of someone
part someone's hair
pass the time
sitting pretty
stick together
walk on eggs

If you have a good dictionary of idioms, you can practice writing clever cards until the cows come home, your ship comes in or until pigs fly. Keep in mind that publishers have a lot of these ideas banked in their files. If you want to succeed in this direction, you need to come up with an entirely new slant or a really new art look that still works with the copy. This kind of writing may seem easy, but in truth, you'll only sell a few. Of course, you're pretty clever and may surpass the odds in this category.

Successful Cute and Clever

In both the cute and the clever categories, you'll find it works well to practice by using old greeting card or magazine art. Often, you'll be given the artwork when you do this kind of assignment. When you don't have art to write to, then you have to look through books or magazines that might spark an idea and use those for inspiration. You can also submit ideas like this with simple stick figure drawings. It is not necessary for you to be an artist as long as you can get your concept across to the editor.

In the next chapter we'll look at the varieties of humor you can write. However, you should have a reasonable understanding of the more traditional side of the greeting card markets and copy styles from the material presented so far. By now you know the importance of collecting materials that will inspire you, being an observer of life and paying attention to what is not being sold in current card lines. You know that you must present a new slant, a new idea or an extremely well-written piece of copy if you hope to publish. The more you approach this kind of writing as a professional writer, the better your results will be.

Remember, too, that there are literally hundreds of small-house publishers who specialize in certain niches in the greeting card market. Research the ones that offer the certain kind of card you want to write and go from there. Companies like Day Spring and Abbey Press will be sources for your religious copy, while publishers like Sunrise and Paramount will welcome your traditional and cute ideas. Just as you do with magazine or book writing, it helps to match your material with the right company. Refer to the most recent *Writer's Market* for a full look at available publishers.

Ways to Improve Your Odds

Try ideas that might spread across three, four or five panels on a card. These can add interest and variety to general card lines. Cards that spread across several panels usually take the format of a rebus, but sometimes they're just related funny pictures, romantic images, beautiful lettering or collages. Sometimes they are pop-outs or scenes. You can create these any way your imagination carries you.

Try writing for specific niche markets like African-American lines or Jewish lines. New direction here is really welcomed by publishers. For help with these markets, notice what current publishers are doing. Hallmark introduced Mahogany to showcase African-American lines. Gibson licenses Gayle and Ardie Sayers and works with a company called Heritage. Several smaller publishers, like Carole Joy and Ethnographics, have become industry leaders in this market. In a focus group that I attended through Gibson, we discovered that buyers of African-American cards are pretty particular about what they want to purchase. Most buyers want the art to depict a black person or to definitely show black culture in one way or another. Most wanted the words to be warm and loving and sentimental. They preferred cards that expressed the real family relationships and beauty of their heritage. This is a market where cute and clever have a chance to grow.

Remember that greeting card writing is not a cookie-cutter procedure. You must constantly keep in mind the recipient and the sending situation of a card. You should always know the reason for a card to exist in the rack and imagine hundreds of people buying into your reason for it. Also, keep in mind that today's publishers often want realism and idealism to walk hand in hand. Even with clever cards, tie into something that just might be true and you will be more successful.

Try your hand at writing cards for pet lovers. Companies are becoming more aware of the increasing importance of pets in people's lives. Today's card racks often offer pet cards that go from your pet to my pet, cards of sympathy in the loss of a pet, cards wishing your pet a merry Christmas or a happy birthday. In most cases, larger companies offer dog and/or cat promotions (special groupings of cards based on a particular art look or subject) on a regular basis. Dog and cat calendars are among the top sellers for most publishers. For some a pet is nearly a member of the family and the greeting card industry doesn't mind adding another family member for you to write a sentiment for. Cute has always worked well in pet cards.

On your next shopping adventure, see if you can find the cute and clever cards and understand the differences. Are there market niches that you might address with these cards?

6 GRINS AND BELLY LAUGHS AND HOW TO GET THEM

If you haven't been doing stand-up comedy or writing jokes for a living, then how do you decide the best way to write humor? What is humor for greeting cards anyway? Well, if you ask six editors or sixty what is funny to them, you'll get six or sixty different perspectives. Humor is always undergoing new definition in the greeting card business. Most companies separate what they call counter humor from alternative humor, and to a lesser degree, studio humor. Actually, some companies are trying to come up with new categories for "edgy" humor because the Shoebox line introduced by Hallmark nearly twenty-five years ago isn't exactly covering the newer alternative directions today. These terms only have meaning in the sense of the markets they are trying to reach.

Counter Humor

Counter humor cards have been attracting baby boomers for over thirty years. They are not usually knee-slapper funny, but they're sendable, fun and sometimes sweet. A counter card should attract the widest audience. Usually, you won't find overly suggestive material or such vulgar slams that you'd be uncomfortable sending the card to your grandmother. (Assumuing your grandmother has a sense of humor.) Counter humor plays off things like parodies and spoofs, die-cut perimeter objects, photos, graphics and cartoons, and topical ideas. Many cards have activity- or interest-related themes.

Parodies and Spoofs

If you take a classic piece like the Mona Lisa and put a mustache and glasses on her in imitation of Groucho Marx, then that's a spoof. You're playing with one well-known image and creating something else. You don't always change it into another well-known piece; it just can happen that way. If you take Rodin's *The Thinker* and put him in a rocking chair, you've spoofed again. Spoofing can be fun, and if you get into it, you may find all kinds of silly things that you never thought to laugh at before.

If you take artwork, famous or otherwise, of a love scene and find a funny way to interpret it, then you've gotten into another spoof situation. You may write a very loving, romantic page 1 to go with the artwork, and then surprise the reader with another whole direction on the inside. We do that sometimes when we show a chimp with kissy lips inside a card that looked very romantic on page 1. When you get a big wet smacker from a chimp, you know you've been spoofed. Here's another example.

FRONT:
Just knowing he was coming soon caused her lips to quiver and her heart to beat a little faster. She planned what she would say and prepared for the moment with sheer delight. This was going to be her moment, her greatest joy in days, this was going to be utterly delectable. The doorbell rang, there he was, she ran to him. . . .

INSIDE:
That'll be $10.99 for the pizza, lady!

TAG LINE:
Hope your wildest fantasies all come true!

Perimeter Objects, Photos, Graphics, Cartoons and Topical Ideas

Die-cut perimeter objects are fun approaches to humor art and copy. Sometimes a clever die cut will look like one thing on the outside of the card and something else on the inside. A die-cut heart, for instance, that opens up to look more like someone's bottom turned upside down makes it more fun to do copy like "I love you from the bottom of my heart."

Photos have gained in popularity over the past few years. Certainly companies like Avanti, Portal and Palm Press have made humorous photos more acceptable industry wide. As a writer, it's a good idea to buy a few of these cards with great photos at your local card retailer and then see what you can do to write new inside copy. When you're still in the store, guess what you think the copy might say. It may not be as easy at it appears. These days computers have made it possible to play with photos in lots of fun ways, so you're seeing more wild and crazy images than you used to.

Bold, graphic illustrated humor is another art approach you can write to. Short, snappy copy will generally be the rule. Sometimes the art will carry these enough that a simple "Happy Birthday" will be the only copy line. Other times, a bold graphic is the best way to add a fun pun. One classic piece shows a cake with hundreds of candles and refers to either the fire department coming or the sprinkler system going off. These are good crossover cards for the hard-to-define older kid and teen market.

Humor cartoons are finding their way into the greeting card racks more than ever. You might see *New Yorker* cartoons in greeting card form, as well as the works of some classic licensed cartoons like *Peanuts*, *Ziggy* and *Cathy*. Character cartoons have their own personality styles, so it's important to study their style and tone before you try to write for them. Yes, you can write for many of them. Make sure you understand Garfield's attitude or Ziggy's life philosophy before you try to send submissions to their creators.

Topical ideas are great in humor but need to be utilized quickly. Industry turnaround times used to be so long that it was difficult to respond to very current fads, but now most publishers have fast-track systems to get those more trendy topics launched. A political cartoonist like Mike Peters is a great guy to watch for topical humor. Follow his cartoons in syndicated columns.

A Wealth of Ideas All Around You

Sources of parodies for your humor writing can come from newspapers, magazines, billboards, posters, yellow pages, TV, radio or the Internet. For example, take the *TV Guide* and write a greeting card called TV Guy. If you can relate all kinds of fun things about Dad on Father's Day that are connected to different TV shows he might watch, then you've created a parody. You've taken something that actually exists and written another version of it to make it funny. Here's a seasonal example: Take a song like "Jingle Bells" and write new words for the same tune. Your new song may be something like "Birthday cake, birthday cake, eat it all the way. Oh, what fun it is to have birthday cake today!" Anyway, whatever version you create, you've written a parody on a well-known song.

Another fun, salable parody uses the personals or the want ads in a new way. For example, the ad shown on the card might read, "Tall, dark, handsome man seeks brilliant and beautiful woman for a night of tender passion and romance." The inside may congratulate the sender's wife on a wedding anniversary, state that all the nights have been wonderful since they've been married, and add that he'd stay home from work if she needed a *day* of passion as well. Car ads and real estate ads offer opportunities for writers as well. Can you come up with a good car ad that will end with a compliment for Father's Day? Can you write a personal ad for the Internet and offer a more contemporary twist?

Consider writing spoofs and parodies of items in your daily mail. Consider the envelopes and what's been scrawled across them, the postage stamps and who or what they're honoring. Write twists on catalogs, bills, letters and, of course, other greeting cards. When you see a funny greeting card, try to guess the punch line before you open it, or give it a new punch line after you read it. Play this game constantly, because there's always another way to look at a setup and punch line, which is what most humor cards are.

You've probably seen cards that play off movies or Broadway show tunes or titles. A card that says something like, "What light through yonder window breaks? Oh, it's your cake!" is just a spoof on Shakespeare with a birthday age gag.

Bookstores can also be a source for ideas. Check the book covers. Do you see any titles that will become more fun if you change one word or phrase? Do you see ways that you can make a funny self-help or how-to card? Glance through the *New York Times* book reviews to find some inspiration. Sometimes the *Reader's Digest* version of a book will give you room to play a new idea or direction. You might even try the children's book section for some cover titles that could have adult applications with some minor twists here and there. Whatever you do, open your mind to the possibilities for new directions in writing greeting card humor. The ball's in your court, so take your best shot.

Examples of Counter Card Humor

This get well card is a parody of a top-ten hit parade.

FRONT:
Here are the TOP TEN tunes in hospitals around the country:
1. *Somebody Stole My Gall*
2. *Seventy-Six Sore Bones*
3. *I've Grown Accustomed to My Gown*
4. *Be Still My Heartburn*
5. *Seems to Me I've Felt This Pain Before*
6. *Has Everybody Seen My Scar?*
7. *I'm Stitched, Bothered and Bewildered*
8. *What Is This Thing Called Lunch?*
9. *I Left My Sponge in San Francisco*
10. *What Now, My Spleen?*

INSIDE:
So why not sing
Your favorite tune
And one more thing—
Please Get Well Soon!

A rebus is a verse in which spot art is used to illustrate the text. Here's an example; can you picture the art?

It's Another Birthday!

There's no way to stall it,
    postpone it, or drop it,
You can't file a lawsuit
    that's able to stop it.
You can't try to trade it,
    suppress it, or waive it,
Or wrap it up tight
    in an effort to save it.
You can't make it
    magically go away—
So just grin and bear it,
    and have a great day!

This spoof incorporates exaggerated language:

May your natal anniversary be permeated by an abundance of jocularity, frivolity and benevolent fraternization . . .

i.e., Have a Happy Birthday

Some cards in the counter line could actually be alternative as well. It mostly depends on the artwork here. This one's an example of a crossover sentiment.

So what if you're another year older?
It's not like you were young last year, either!
Happy Birthday

78

What Is Alternative Humor?

Alternative humor started when the smaller houses developed inexpensive, single-fold cards with limited artwork, no special finishes and a simple funny joke. These cards inspired the *Shoebox* line from Hallmark, *78th Street* from American Greetings and *Neat Stuff* and then *Life as We Know It* and *Ripple Effects* from Gibson. All the companies tried to do a basic pen-and-ink concept, with up-to-date funny lines that would grab younger consumers. Some of these cards didn't even correspond to a sending situation. They were just funny.

Alternative cards tend to use more topical humor than counter cards. They can offer political humor, celebrity references, celebrity images, current events, current phrases and trendy stuff or fads. These cards try to be up-to-the-minute and appeal to a fairly well-read and well-educated audience. Some companies will push these cards to the edge with sexual or suggestive humor, using words that would have once been deemed inappropriate for greeting cards. Gibson Greetings developed a line in 1997 called *Ripple Effects.*

Gary Larson's cards featuring *The Far Side* cartoons were a hit, even though they often had no real me-to-you sentiment. Nonoccasion cards had been around before, but this development, now nearly twenty-five years old, really revived the market. Many small companies have sprung up in the past twenty-five years and many of them thrive on this formula of low-cost cards with simple designs and no finishes. It's a formula that seems to be holding its own. And even though alternative cards are once again undergoing a metamorphosis, if you can write good, funny lines, then you should find a niche in a number of publishing houses today. The new alternative lines are yet to be defined. Perhaps you will help guide the publishers to a new era in quick, funny punch lines. Let's look at some examples of current alternative cards.

This verse comes from the *Ripple Effects* line and is shown with artwork of people partying.

FRONT:

In honor of your birthday, we're all going out for drinks after work.

INSIDE:
Just wanted to let you know in case we get in late tomorrow.

Picture a snarling, mean looking dog here.

FRONT:
In this dog-eat-dog world, it's nice to know I have a friend like you.

INSIDE:
Someone who's not a dog, and as far as I know, has never eaten a dog.

Picture a man with a deadpan expression and cake on his face.

FRONT:
When you were little it used to be so cute how you'd dig into the birthday cake with your fingers and get it all over your face.

INSIDE:
It's not cute anymore.
It grosses everyone out.

Picture a portly man attempting to pull up his pants.

FRONT:
Another birthday?
I bet if you tried to put on a pair of pants you wore back in high school, you couldn't get them up past your knees.

INSIDE:
Which, from what I hear, is where they were most of the time anyway.

Alternative humor cards mostly cover current topics and tend to be slightly irreverent and edgy in their approach. If you like this kind of writing, you're in great shape because publishers are all looking for good writers for this market. How suggestive you go with these is something you and the publisher have to decide. I have a personal preference in that I still like a greeting card to be something you don't have to hide under the bed so the kids don't see it, but that's just me. The market seems to bear most anything. Here are some relatively edgy examples.

Picture a woman on a sofa and children hanging from the walls and ceiling.

> FRONT:
> *Once she discovered Velcro, Marge found she had a lot more free time.*
>
> INSIDE:
> *Wishing you a quiet, restful Mother's Day.*

The accompanying art for this verse should be easy to imagine.

> FRONT:
> *For Your Birthday*
> *Tonight while you sleep, little elves will vacuum and dust, clean the bathroom, do the laundry, shop for groceries and have breakfast ready when you wake up!*
>
> INSIDE:
> *Why not? It works for men.*

Here's a racier card.

> FRONT:
> *I'd like to run away with you to a small hotel on the Riviera!*
>
> INSIDE:
> *Or a small pup tent in the Rockies . . . or a furnace room in my basement . . . or. . . .*

81

This verse incorporates political humor and accompanies a caricature of Ross Perot by Mike Peters.

> FRONT:
> *Here comes that giant sucking sound . . .*
>
> INSIDE:
> *Birthdays suck!*

This woman-to-woman card depicts a guy in a convertible driving down a country road while a cow watches him go by.

> FRONT:
> *Just think—at this very minute, Mr. Right is trying to find you.*
>
> INSIDE:
> *But of course, he won't ask for directions.*

Here's a nonoccasion friendship card.

> FRONT:
>
> *This friend is too boring*   (shows person and dog
>   sleeping)
> *And this friend is too weird.* (shows character dressed like
>   clown)
> *But you . . .*
>
> INSIDE:
> *You're just boring and weird enough.*

This humorous nonoccasion card is blank inside for your own message.

A cartoon by Mike Peters of two doe and one buck at a bar accompanies the caption:

*You're asking for trouble Joyce. . . . Look at his ear. . . .
He's been tagged.*

Here's another suggestive card.

FRONT:
Please take good care of yourself.

INSIDE:
There are parts of you I'm not finished with yet.

Pets and relationships, woman-to-woman gripes and griefs, and just about anything that you can poke fun at or slam makes good alternative humor. Photographs are a good way to work on your writing for this market. Pull them from ads, your family album, CD covers, news services, stockhouse catalogs and anywhere else you might find them. The main thing is attitude. Whatever the topic, the card has to pull off a lifestyle-oriented, high-attitude approach.

Gary Morgan, an excellent humor editor/writer, gave me some tips to pass along to you.

A funny gag isn't enough! The best greeting cards still need to relate to some occasion and should have some relevance to the sender and receiver. Even in humor, you need to think about who's buying the card and who's receiving it. Would they really enjoy what your card says? Find a way to tie your card to a birthday or a holiday and make it more fun.

A 5 to 10 percent acceptance rate is average, so if you send in twenty ideas and only sell one, you're doing just fine. Likewise, if you receive a note that says "have similar" or "an industry standard," it just means that you're on track, but someone else got there ahead of you. Don't settle for the first good punch line you come up with; keep twisting and turning it until you are certain you've got the best one.

What Are Studio Cards?

The tall, slender cards you see in the racks are known as studio cards, which started in the 1950s and were formula-driven with setups and punch lines. They often got rather naughty, and even today you'll have to work with the editor to determine where to draw the line on these. When these cards started out, they drew on a more cynical approach to life at the close of World War II.

Years ago, I was giving a talk to a group of Shriners in the Cleveland area. When we started to talk about the history of greeting cards, the whole room was able to repeat lines from some of their favorite studio cards, like "Candy is dandy, but liquor is quicker" and the card with the big water droplet on the front that said, "Drop . . . dead!" Whew! Talk about cynical! These were not love cards by any stretch of the imagination. One of the wonderful things about the greeting card industry is that it grows and changes with the times and the culture. That's why you'll find it immensely challenging to keep up with today's culture because the information age has brought change so quickly that most of us find our heads spinning.

I suggest you take a good look at studio humor in the racks and get a feel for the topics being addressed there today. For the most part, these cards are rather edgy, sometimes biting and seldom sweet. Studio humor is still successful and comes in a wide variety of formats. Hallmark now has several sizes for these cards. Most publishers still use the old recognizable tall, thin studio size format.

A Closer Look at Rebus Cards

Backtracking a bit, let's take a closer look at rebus cards. The rebus is a classic "bread and butter" humor approach that won't die quickly in the greeting card business. Gary Morgan has offered several tips that you should consider when writing a rebus.

- Make sure your card has a theme or topic that a recipient will be able to relate to throughout the card. For example:

  Moms are like books, flowers, desserts, etc.

  There are all kinds of brothers, sisters, uncles, etc.

*I love you when you're happy, I love you when you're sad,
I love you when . . .*

- A rebus is not a collection of random thoughts and rhymes. Each line should stay true to the topic and continue to develop one main idea. Don't try to put a variety of topics into one card.
- A rebus should build lines or couplets that are easy to illustrate.
- The rebus should have a summary statement that pulls all the parts together for the recipient and expresses a theme like love or a compliment.
- Today's rebus should use contemporary language and avoid facile "true/you" rhyme. Use elements in the rebus that make it clear this verse was written in the present and not twenty years ago. Editors find that writers tend to continue the tried-and-true approaches. Be open to some exploration here and give the industry some new stuff.
- Be aware that the majority of rebus verses should avoid the use of *I* or *We* so that the card has greater sendability. Of course, if it has a love theme, it may need an *I* verse, but general categories need general themes that can be sold to anyone.
- Rebuses employ a light humor. You aren't out for belly laughs here. Most of the time, you are reminding the sender and receiver of some shared experience or sweet memory. Generally, the rebus wraps up with a feel-good sentiment for the recipient.
- The length of a rebus can be four lines, eight lines or more. Your part is to make sure it all hangs together and, like any good story, has reasonable transitions. The reader can make some associative leaps with you, but can't read your mind. You have to show how you get from one thought to the next.
- Though rebus writing has been rather imaginative and whimsical in the past, the industry is seeking more real-life situations for these cards. Reliving fun experiences with the family or from childhood may be just the thing to inspire your writing. Maybe a jog down memory lane with your own family

would help give you some ideas about a shared experience universal enough to make a good rebus greeting card.

Some Rebus Examples
This card has fun with 1960s slang.

> *You'd probably laugh if I said you were GROOVY,*
> *And PEACHY just sounds like a beach party movie.*
> *NIFTY's as dated as hot rods and malt shops,*
> *And no one's said FAB since the Beatles were mop tops.*
> *Although some expressions fade after a while—*
> *GREAT people like you NEVER go OUT OF STYLE!*

The imagery in the above rebus is based on shared memories. In the following verse, all the details ring true as things a father could teach his son.

> *You taught me how to throw a ball*
> *And how to change a tire,*
> *You taught me how to fix a leak*
> *And grill steaks on the fire.*
> *You taught me how to stand up straight*
> *And make myself look taller,*
> *But the BEST thing that you taught me, DAD . . .*
> (hand holding dollar bill which stretches as slider opens)
> *. . . is how to stretch a dollar!*

Here's one that begins with an indirect observation, then personalizes it for the conclusion.

> *Some women have a thing for men*
> *Whose names are up in lights . . .*
> *Some dream of kings . . .*
> *Or millionaires . . .*
> *Some yearn for gallant knights . . .*
> *Some think the sports world's hunks*
> *Are all as sexy as can be . . .*

But I go wild for just one man—
The one who married me!

The traditional comparison rebus uses simile and metaphor to carry the card through a series of thoughts about a related object. This style is still effective when done well. Keep in mind that every line must tie into the subject.

Dads Are Like Cars

Some are sporty,
Some have style—
Some are cool,
Some make you smile—
Some are classics,
Some are new—
But special ones
Like YOU are few!

Happy Father's Day, Dad!

It's best if you can avoid ending verse with you/too/few/true/etc. Here's a classic rebus that avoided the *oo* rhyme problem.

To My Wife With Love on Valentine's Day

I've seen you at your very best,
I've seen you at your worst . . .
I've seen you warm and loving
And so angry you could burst . . .
I've seen you happy,
Seen you sad—
but let me state this clearly . . .
I've never, ever seen you
When I didn't love you dearly!

Here's a rebus for an active, contemporary grandmother.

87

Some grandmothers paint with colorful oils,
Some grandmothers cook and make sure nothing spoils,
Some grandmothers read daring books of romance,
Some grandmothers love and chance for a dance,
Yes, grandmothers find lots of fun things to do,
But, Grandma, there's no one who's more fun than you.

 IDEA
JOGGER

What can you do to get those fun(ny) ideas flowing? For starters, you can try some silly alliteration or simple clichés.

Five funny fisherman flipped and floated forever.
Eight gray geese grazed grandly in Greece.
Write is right unless it's wrong and should be rite.

Starting with some of these lead lines you can rephrase Murphy's Law (if anything can go wrong, it will) or put a twist on an old proverb.

You can fool some of the people . . .
If you're feeling good . . .
If you do something you think everyone will like . . .
Never open a can of worms unless . . .
An ounce of prevention is worth . . .
Good judgment comes from . . .
If you eat spaghetti in a white shirt . . .

Search all sorts of different sources for quotes and rewrite them. For example, this famous Henny Youngman line, "Take my wife . . . please!" has been quoted thousands of times. Can you come up with a line that's so easy to fall into?

Find a fun way to twist and turn any of the following quotes into a new idea and then into a me-to-you kind of greeting card.

> We regret we are unable to give you the weather. We rely on weather reports from the airport, which is closed because of the weather. Whether we are able to give you the weather tomorrow depends on the weather.
> —Arab News

> Learn this and you'll get along, no matter what your situation: An ounce of keep-your-mouth-shut beats a ton of explanation.
> —Anonymous

> You can't depend on your eyes when your imagination is out of focus.
> —Mark Twain

Humor-Writing Tips
From Angela Walsh, an assistant editor at Gibson:

> The funniest cards are often a direct result of our everyday experiences. People find humor in things they can really relate to—being a parent, dating, common pet peeves, etc. But it's not a matter of formulating a joke. The trick is to take these experiences and combine them with an appropriately funny me-to-you message.

From humor writer Gary Morgan:

> Because senses of humor are so varied, there is no magic formula that can tell us whether an idea is going to be a hit. We can rely on observation of competition, historical success and editorial experience, but even so, the wide range of tastes in humor still presents an unpredictable factor.

Improving Your Chances of Making a Sale

I've given you an overview of the types of greeting card humor and
how to understand what publishers might look for. Humor markets
have changed and publishers are pushing for edgier and more up-
to-the-minute topics. Here are some clues that might help you in
today's market.

- Surprise me! Don't telegraph the contents of the card too
  quickly on the front. Let the buyer and the recipient be surprised at what the card says. Here's an example of a sentiment
  you probably wouldn't expect when you picked up the card.

  > FRONT:
  > *Roses are red,*   (yes, I said not to use this format, but
  > *Violets are blue,* there are exceptions to every guideline I
  >   could give you)

  > INSIDE:
  > *Sunflowers are yellow, grass is green, bananas are also*
  > *yellow, poop is brown, Captain Kirk's shirt is sort of yel-*
  > *lowish, earwax is like a beige-gold color, spackling paste*
  > *is white, red underwear is red, as is Gilligan's shirt, those*
  > *great big purple things are purple, the Black Death was*
  > *black, as is the Black Hole of Calcutta, peanut butter and*
  > *jelly is brownish and purplish, respectively, eye goop is*
  > *mostly clear—by the way—Happy Valentine's Day.*

  I know you didn't expect it to say all that on the inside!

- And this just in! Hot off the press! Up to the minute! Big companies and small ones are constantly trying to come up with
  ways to get current material into the market a whole lot faster.
  They work hard to shorten turnaround times, so don't assume
  that you won't have time to get an idea to market. Companies
  are scrambling to get today's news out there *today*.
- This may go without saying, but I'll risk it. Be funnier! The
  cards that have the best shot in any humor market are the
  funny ones. Cute is good, clever is better, but funny is best! If

you want to sell your stuff, try it out on a few willing souls and find out if they think it's funny. Never send anything into a publisher that you don't think is good. If you wouldn't buy it, why should they?

- Now, along with being funny, be unique! Look at what you've written and try to come up with another format for the same joke. Would it work just as well as a rebus? Would it work better as a limerick? Could you turn it around and have it still make sense or make it even funnier? The obvious answer is not always the best answer. Try the next one or the one after that to get a really good piece of copy. You might just find the punch line gets funnier as you keep punching it.

- Develop an attitude. Most of the edgy humor today expresses some kind of attitude. Mike Peters's dog, Grimmy, is a dog with an attitude. Jim Davis's cat, Garfield, has had an attitude for years and is still popular. Your writing needs to reflect the attitudes of current thinking and trends. If you're writing Generation X kind of stuff, then search the market and find out what prevailing attitudes are. An attitude isn't necessarily good or bad, it's just a reflection of the culture and a mirror of how people think in a certain segment of society.

- Pay attention to which cards yell at you from the rack, "Pick me up! Read me! I dare you!" If you're like most people, the cards with fun visuals will grab your attention first. Sometimes it's color impact, and sometimes it's funky lettering styles, but the artwork is important to getting the point across and selling that card. When you write humor, try to imagine the artwork as well. Give it a graphic from a magazine or some clip art from your computer. Attention-grabbing visuals help make cards jump off the rack, and any ideas you can recommend to the editor will help sell your words too.

What Tools Do You Need?

You need a good sense of humor, and you need to know how to deliver a funny line. As in stand-up comedy, timing is everything. If you telegraph the message too quickly, it won't be funny. If you take too long to get to the punch line, your reader will have put the card back already. You have to have that sense of timing, and you have to know what people think is funny. A good joke book might help you get started. Classic comedy ideas could help too, but probably just reading the racks will give you the best sense of this market and help you get started writing good humor.

It also helps to be a magazine fanatic because there's a wealth of material to be gleaned from the ads and the stories. All types of magazines exist because people have a wide variety of interests. Just reading the names will give you ideas for spin-offs that might make fun greeting cards.

If you're a computer person, then learning to manipulate images on the computer can give you new ideas for copy directions. Access to the Internet is also helpful because you can lock on to all those greeting card sites and read tons of card ideas without leaving your home. Hallmark, American Greetings, Greet Street and some other publishers all have Web sites that will give you plenty of mental exercise. Most of the prominent cartoonists also have Web sites, and you'll get more information there. Try www.shoebox.com /funny/card/. This Hallmark site lists copy ideas that earned the response, "Funny, but no." According to the site, the card ideas here were either too weird, too off-color or too much of a stretch. The site www.grimmy.com will give you a look at how Mike Peters develops *Mother Goose and Grimm*. These and other Web sites will give you more help in understanding the humor market.

Mike Peters offered the following reflection on writing humor.

I love greeting cards. I love being able to communicate with people through my artwork, and creating cards is a unique way of communicating. It's a different way to be able to reach out to people, and that's what I like about it. My tip: Keep a "blip book." Read greeting cards to keep up with trends. I take a notepad and pencil when I read cards at the store. I'll write down key words or phrases that are funny or that stand out—trendy stuff! Later, I'll look back on those words and phrases to help me think of good card ideas.

Mike Peters definitely is an idea guy, and those who write for his character learn to look for the trendy, the funny and that little extra surprise inside a card. The payoff comes from the surprise, the part of the card that really makes you laugh. You can see in the illustration of Grimm below that a surprise factor is just what the copy should provide with the artwork. Can you come up with a good inside line for it?

© Grimmy Inc.

Reprinted by permission of Grimmy, Inc. © Grimmy, Inc.

If you don't have a specific assignment from a company, give yourself a special writing project, such as animal puns. Since this is an established part of the industry, writing new, solid directions for this is a challenge. You'll have to go beyond the obvious because you can be sure those have been done many times already, but new ones must be out there. What puns can you think of for a panda? An alligator? A spot-checker, a henpecker or a ring-necker? If you can tune a piano but you can't tuna fish, then this kind of writing is for you. (P.S. Thanks to Caroline for that one.)

You might try a subject matter project like fishing or sailing or golf. These are popular subjects of greeting card art and new lines are needed to keep them fresh and interesting. Other areas might be themes like country music, travel humor or toys. Pick a topic that you see everywhere and fill it with as many funny verses as you can. It's also good to do writing projects around various greeting card occasions too, such as birthdays, Valentine's Day, Christmas and Mother's Day. These are always being addressed in the marketplace, and your input could gain sales for you.

If you have some time, I suggest a trip to your local art museum. What can you find there? Well you can take the images you see and turn them into funny or off-the-wall spoofs. You can have an elderly lady putting sweaters on nudes to keep them warm, or you could put earplugs on *The Scream*. As you wander the gallery, you're sure to find many visuals that will spark ideas.

Use the standard humor formats (double meaning, exaggeration, incongruity, etc.) to poke fun at people, and keep on creating. Try not to focus so much on needing a valentine piece as needing a funny bit for lovers or friends. The more you think about the recipient or the situation, the more salable your piece will be. And remember, the best humor is always a little bit true.

Humorous Copy Assessment

Sometimes publishers conduct an in-house test of their own humor copy to try to get an idea about whether a piece will make it out in the marketplace. The following pieces were part of such a test. The questions asked about each sentiment were: Do you think this card is funny? Would you buy it? If not, why not? Ask yourself those questions before you submit any work to a publisher.

This one earned a big YES. The front of the card depicts a dark room with these words in bright letters:

FRONT:
Ohhhhh . . . Ohhhhh!
You still fill my nights with spine-tingling excitement!

INSIDE:
Please, quit leaving the toilet seat up.

The majority of the people reading this card really liked it. Most of them were women.

Here's another one that tested well.

FRONT:
Happy Birthday!
The good news is you're still sexy enough to wear a see-through nightgown.

INSIDE:
The bad news is you don't know anyone who can still see through it.

The good news/bad news setup is one you might try in your own writing. It is still a very acceptable formula for humorous cards.

Here's one that didn't test well and therefore didn't get purchased or published.

FRONT:
I think of you so often. Of course, you couldn't know that, because I never tell you, because I'm a real jerk about keeping in touch, and I really feel bad about being such a crummy, rotten friend.

INSIDE:
How come every time I think of you I get depressed?

Why do you think this one didn't work? Self-deprecating humor is standard in the industry, but in this case it goes so far that it isn't funny anymore. A word like "jerk" may be considered too harsh and mislead the reader. In this case, I don't think the sender or the receiver would have any fun with this card.

Examples of Seasonal Needs Lists

Before we end this humor section, it might be helpful to get a peek at a real needs list. Editors present these in a variety of ways. Some are pretty straightforward and some are more playful. Personally, I think the playful ones are more apt to get you into the mood to write.

Gary Morgan of Gibson Greetings wrote this Easter list like a news bulletin. "EASTER EGG TRAGEDY: BUNNY CRACKS UNDER STRESS!" He goes on to explain that maybe the bunny didn't, but he might if *he* doesn't get good material from freelancers. He divided the list into several categories.

> **Alternative General:** Suitable for sending by anyone to anyone. Topics should be related to everyday life situations, or take a familiar part of Easter and turn it inside out. Themes can be simple Wish, a Compliment, Thinking of You, Advice or Observations. Remember to have a solid me-to-you message as well. Avoid religious references that could offend.
>
> **Alternative Love:** Should be sendable by either loved one. Nothing too randy, please.
>
> **Humorous Counter Captions:** Rhyme and unrhymed ideas are welcome for any of these.
>
> **Honey:** Need Love, Compliment and How Much You Mean themes that can be sent by either sex. Avoid limiting to marriage situations.
>
> **Husband:** Need Love and Compliment themes. Avoid limiting the age or sex of sender. (Wish should be sincere, but without excess emotion.)
>
> **Daughter:** Need Love or Compliment themes. Avoid limiting daughter's age. She could be a teen at home or a wife and mother. Try to avoid saying "I" or "We."

From this needs list, you can learn what caption areas are most needed in the Easter humor line. You can also get a better understanding of alternative and counter lines and what themes are used most often. When editors point out the limitations they are trying to avoid, be sure to consider those when you write. Many times good writing is rejected because it is not widely sendable. Since many greeting cards are published in runs of twenty to thirty thousand, you can understand the need for very sendable verses that appeal to a lot of people.

Don't Forget About Kid Humor

Humor is an excellent way to get through to the older, preteen kid category. Don't forget to keep it contemporary. *Cool* is a good word, but there must be others that would make a kid feel good and "with it." Sometimes there's a chance to make up a word, as in "you're a wonderfantertifulastic kid." Keep in mind that pop-ups and other gimmicks might work well here too, but you should keep them fun and current. Greeting card companies have historically done pretty well with younger recipients, but this area of older kids and teens still needs you. In fact, all the way through college ages, humor is a great vehicle. Remembering all we've discussed here should help you excel in this market.

7 HOW DO I GET A CARD COMPANY TO LOOK AT MY WRITING?

In greeting card writing, like any other writing, you need to find a way to get your foot in the door. Having a connection helps, but it's not necessary. Most of the time, you can follow a procedure like this.

You can read *Writer's Market* or some other guide that gives you names of companies to write to. Search the Internet to find the names of publishers and what they look for, and consider attending the annual Stationery Show in New York City. Once you have a list of publishers you are interested in, you can send a query to ask if they accept freelance writing and ask for writer's guidelines and/or needs lists. Typically, they'll send guidelines, sometimes the needs list and some kind of disclosure form so you can declare that you want them to actually look at your work. In a lawsuit-happy world, companies are becoming less willing to just open mail as it comes in. If your name isn't on the roster of freelance writers they use, they will probably send your work back unopened.

Once you've signed the disclosure form and returned it, I suggest you send a letter that states your experience in the industry and why you're interested in this kind of writing. If you have no experience, then you might say that you have been writing poetry and stories since you were a child and you think this kind of writing is something you'll enjoy. They'll probably give you a chance to see what you can do. If it fits into their publishing plans, they may also send you a writing test to determine what your skill level really is.

When you get the needs list, study it carefully. Go to stores and look at the types of materials you are being asked to write so that you can understand the feel and direction of what that company publishes. If you can't find a retail outlet or store display for the publisher you're sending material to, call and ask where you might see the publisher's products. They'll give you the address of the store nearest to you. If all else fails, at least go to a card shop and read the same category you're being asked to write. By category, I mean all the birthday cards or all the wedding cards or all the Halloween cards. Immerse yourself in the types of cards you're being asked for so you can imitate while avoiding what's already there. Again I urge you to look for lead lines or words that you feel drawn to on a card and find a different way to express that idea, or write a new inside line.

Many social expression publishers use Hallmark as a gauge, and you can too. When you're satisfied that you know how and what to do, check the needs list carefully for industry words you might not understand. Call and clarify things with the publisher if you need to, and then get busy writing. At this point, you are trying to write at least one good sentiment that the editor will like. It's good to submit two ideas for the same item requested to give you a better chance of hitting it. If the needs list is open-ended and no specific card is being requested, then send ten to fifteen ideas for the category. Sometimes if I'm on a roll and the needs list requests several cards for a dad's birthday, I'll send as many as I can write. When you're new to a publisher, however, I think you should pace yourself and send only your very best material. Sending a huge batch makes you memorable sometimes, but not always in a positive way.

An editor would rather receive five solid sentiments than twenty "OK, but we've got them already" pieces.

Submitting Your Material

To give yourself the best opportunity for making sales, ask yourself these questions before you submit material.

1. Have I selected the best publisher for this material?
2. Could I expand this card idea into a series of cards?
3. Is this idea original? Unique? Why?
4. Is this idea timely? Does it have universal appeal?
5. Do I have a particular art look in mind? Should I send a picture or draw a stick figure?
6. Would I buy this card?
7. Would this idea work for a different type of product? Calendars? Plaques? Stickers? Mugs? Posters? T-shirts?

Check every sentiment to make sure that each word is meaningful. When you write very short copy, each word counts. Actually, when you write anything for publication, each word counts, but it's even more true in greeting card writing. If you find words that are just fillers, change them or delete them. If you find words that are too lofty or too stilted, work on them. Create every piece so that you feel proud of it. If you do, you'll feel good about your work whether it's purchased or not.

Make sure each sentiment is properly typed. Your presentation is important. Editors prefer to work with professional writers. Punctuation and clear, concise writing will keep you on the editor's list.

Make sure you send me-to-you sentiments and not poetry. Poetry may have a place in the greeting card world, but typically it's better submitted to a magazine.

Make sure you number each sentiment. It helps you and the editor when choices are made. Editors will usually reference those numbers when sending you a letter stating what pieces they wish to purchase.

Do not send material simultaneously to more than one publisher. Sometimes your piece will fit an immediate need, and if you've sent it to other publishers too, things get complicated and you may lose the sale.

Only send original material. Don't recap a TV show and try to send the idea as your own unless you've really created a new concept for your greeting card. Sometimes, you'll see something and remember it and even type it as your own, but that should be a very rare occurrence.

Send material in a timely manner. If the editor gives you a due date, stick to it. Deadlines are important when work is needed for an upcoming card promotion. The more reliable you are, the more requests you'll receive.

Put your name and address on the back of each piece you submit. Sometimes pieces get separated from a particular batch and it's much easier to return if you've labeled each one. It helps to date the material too, so that you and the editor can keep track of how old the submission is.

If you don't know the editor's name, then send your work to the writing manager, the humor editor or the seasonal editor. The closer you get to submitting to the right person, the more likely your work will be given proper consideration.

Check your submission for up-to-date language. If you've used old-fashioned words like *grand* or *folks* or *impart/heart*, then give your sentiment some more thought.

Make sure you've done your homework so that you submit the right material to the right publisher. This is especially important when you submit work to Christian publishers who only accept certain styles.

Do not send handwritten submissions. Either type your words or create them on your computer. Your submission should look something like this:

FRONT:
Sure hope you know how much you mean . . .

INSIDE:
. . . each month, each year and in between!

Send illustrations only if they enhance the understanding of your writing. Editors do not expect you to send artwork. Sometimes a stick figure can help a humor piece make sense to the editor, however.

A Word About Faxed Material

If you're under contract, that's one thing, but if you're just freelancing, check with the editors about how they feel about faxing. Yes, you can fax material to a publisher, but I don't recommend it unless you're requested to do so. It's much more difficult to keep good records when you batch several pieces on one sheet and fax it. It's harder for the publisher, too, because if they want one piece off your list, they run the risk of losing one tiny strip of paper that they may have cut to attach to a purchase order. Even if you fax material, you should send a response envelope if you want the material returned. Certainly in the near future you'll be able to submit work right off the Internet or through E-mail and no paper will be required. Companies do this now, but I don't believe it protects you or the company as well as hard copy submissions.

Copyrights for Greeting Cards

First, those of us who have worked in this industry want you to be comfortable with the fact that any professional publisher is *not* going to steal your ideas. I have heard people express the concern that a company might take their ideas and not pay them. If such a thing ever occurred in the past, I apologize for the whole industry, but I don't think you'll ever find that a concern today. Although many ideas come in from several contributors that are very similar, they will obviously only purchase one of the similar ideas. If you see it on a card rack later, that is most likely what happened. Though we all like to think we are incredibly original, the truth is, many ideas occur almost simultaneously because writers tap into similar information and resources.

Typically it is not necessary for freelance writers to register their work. According to an article by Howard G. Zaharoff published in the May 1996 *Writer's Digest*:

> Copyright law protects the way an author or artist expresses an idea or concept, but does not protect the underlying ideas or concepts themselves.

Typically, a greeting card is copyrighted by simply putting a *c* inside a circle (the copyright symbol), the year and your name. For example, I might write © 1998 Karen Moore. Usually, a publisher will buy *all rights* to your piece, which means they own it and you cannot sell it to any other greeting card publisher. There are times when I have cautioned people to consider a submission further before agreeing to those terms. For instance, if you write a beautiful little story that will be published on a greeting card for children but might be something you should actually submit to a children's book publisher, you may not want to sell it to a card manufacturer. You'll get more mileage out of it with the book publisher. I realize this won't happen all that often, but some greeting card companies do publish some pretty lengthy material that might just as appropriately be of interest to a book publisher. Once you've sold it to a card publisher, you usually can't sell it again. Electronic media is a new ball game for copyright gurus, so stay posted and ask questions if you're submitting work over the Internet.

Keeping Your Work Organized

Keep a master file—either a regular card file or a notebook, but something you know is a definitive reference of what you sent and where you sent it. It's probably easier to keep a record on your computer. Basically, you need to know which company you sent a piece to, when you mailed it, when you received it back and whether it was rejected or accepted. If it was accepted, how much did you get paid for it? Keep track. The IRS will expect to hear from you if you earn enough money. You'll want to file a Schedule C tax form as a freelance writer. Check the latest tax information rules regarding your freelance life to learn up front what receipts to keep, what capital expenses you may have and what is expected of you if you develop your freelance business. Most companies you work for will not withhold tax payments from your checks, so you'll need to pay your taxes on a regular basis yourself. Make sure you keep detailed records. The beauty of only submitting one idea per card or per page is that you can keep your records cleaner.

Once a piece is returned to you without acceptance, submit it to the next publisher. Make sure you always enclose a SASE (self-addressed stamped envelope) because the company should not have to pay you to return your work. Some companies simply will not return unsolicited material without it. If your work was solicited, you need to be even more aware of approaching the company in a professional manner. They'll send you more assignments if you follow the rules.

Now that you have a master file in a notebook, computer file or in a file drawer, determine a numbering system and a code for each company you're submitting material to. If possible, keep your ideas filed under the *type* (birthday, Christmas, anniversary, etc.) so when material is returned, you can find it more easily when another request comes in. Set up whatever code and numbering system makes sense to you. Make it easy, though, so that you can easily remember what each symbol means. Try something like this:

SENTIMENT #	COMPANY	DATE SENT	DATE RETURNED	PURCHASED	COMMENTS
B640	Hallmark	5/20	6/20	No	"Have Similar"
B640	American Greetings	7/1	8/5	No	No comment

CODES:	B: BIRTHDAY
	H: HALLOWEEN
	C: CHRISTMAS
	F: FRIENDSHIP

In the above example, you have submitted sentiment B640. You have a sentiment with that number on a file card or in the computer. You've submitted it twice and received two rejections. One came back with a comment and one didn't. What do you do next? Check the sentiment again to see if it's as clear and as professional as it can be, and then resubmit it, of course! I want to emphasize that it's always better not to send simultaneous submissions. One company at a time should have the opportunity to review your work. Keep a list of where you want to send it next if it is rejected so that you're ready to turn it around and get it back in the mail as soon as possible.

Checking on Your Material

If you submitted material two months ago and you haven't heard a word, then you should feel free to contact the publisher and ask for a status report. If you only sent it in two weeks ago, then it's probably too soon to get feedback. Often, the editor for a line will collect all the freelance materials for a few weeks and then take them to a review committee for final approval. Your material may go through several screenings before purchases are actually made. It always takes longer for a freelancer to get feedback than one would like, but try to have patience and realize that a lot of things are going on with the publisher, and most of them have little to do with your work. Publishers will usually get back to you in a reasonable time. Some publishers that do take several months to hold and purchase your material will tell you in advance that their system is lengthy. It's up to you whether you want to submit material to them. Try to get an editor's name as soon as you can so you know who to contact when you do have questions.

Keeping Careful Records

It's helpful to keep records so you can build up a track record with your publishers. If you know who bought what and how often, you'll be able to make a case for getting a freelance contract. Freelance contracts are not easy to find, but if you have been successful and sold many pieces to one publisher, you may pitch the idea to them. Make sure you can meet the weekly quotas for usable material, however. Contract writers have to hit more often than general freelancers if they hope to keep their positions. It's also very helpful to remember where you sent material and avoid seeming unprofessional by sending the same material back to a publishing house that has already reviewed it. Occasionally, a publisher will request you submit your sentiments again later, but only do that when requested.

Getting Rejected

Most of us do not really become immune to rejection, but we learn to understand why editors say no to our material. In the greeting card industry, you can expect rejection for the following reasons.

- You're material is too similar to some copy they already have in their file.
- It doesn't fit the need they have at the moment.
- The writing style is not one they use.
- You've submitted an industry classic.
- You need to do more homework so that you understand the kind of material they really buy. It won't take long to discover that you can't send Blue Mountain Arts the same material you would send to Oatmeal Studios.
- Your piece does not hang together well.
- The editor does not really understand what your piece is saying.
- The piece is OK, but it is too hard to think of a way to illustrate it.
- The piece contains some word or phrase that would require legal consideration.
- You need to polish the piece more and then send it back.

There may be other reasons, but I think these are the most likely ones. More often than not, timing is another important factor to your sales. If you submit when the budget for freelance work is almost used up, editors will be more picky about what they buy. If you happen to send material close on the heels of some recent purchases then timing is the problem again. It's best to nurture a relationship with two or three companies and get to know their needs and interests than to go after too many publishers at once.

8 YOUR WORKBOOK

Traditional Rhymed Verse

When most people think of greeting card writing, they imagine
something like this.

> On Your Birthday
>
> *You're a wonderful person*
> *Who's so nice to know*
> *'Cause you make people happy*
> *Wherever you go.*
> *It's no wonder you're wished*
> *All the best things there are,*
> *And the happiest birthday*
> *That you've had so far!*
>
> *Have a Great Birthday!*

Of all the types of greeting card writing available today, the traditional eight-line rhymed verse remains the most popular and best-
selling form.

Write an eight-line rhymed verse for a brother's birthday. Make the message warm and assume a close relationship, even if the two people involved do not live near each other. Here's an example.

> *It's great to have a brother*
> *Who's a mover and shaker,*
> *A brother who's much more*
> *Of a giver than a taker,*   (a compliment)
> *It's great to just remember*
> *The joys that we've shared*   (close relationship)
> *'Cause a brother like you*
> *Just couldn't be compared.*

EXERCISE 2
Short Prose

Greeting card messages often express one simple thought in a warm and direct way. Since these messages generally go with many art styles, they can be used over and over again. The key is to say exactly what the card sender wanted to relate to the recipient.

> *Any time I stop to think about our friendship,*
> *I realize what a difference you have made*
> *in my life. Thanks for being there*
> *when I need you.*

Write a short prose message for each of the sending situations listed below. An example is included for each.

1. Son on his birthday

> *A son like you always fills the family*
>   *with love and pride. Today, more than ever*
>   *you're wished every happiness.*

2. A husband expressing love to his wife, no special occasion

I hope you know that no one means more to me
than you do, and I wouldn't want
to spend a day or a night without you by my side.
I love you more than I could ever say.

EXERCISE 3
The Most Universal Message

Greeting cards publishers receive all kinds of freelance material. For this exercise, let's assume you have to choose just one sentiment that should be published. Base your decision on the sentiment that you feel will appeal to the widest number of people and explain why you made that choice. What were the limits imposed by the sentiments you did not choose?

1. *Wishing you sunshine and rainbows*
   and all the things that make your birthday
   warm and bright.
2. *When I think of all you've been through,*
   I can't help but wish you
   brighter days ahead
   on your birthday and always.
3. *Along with warmest wishes*
   for your happiness today,
   This greeting brings a prayer
   that's offered in a heartfelt way,
   A prayer that God will grant you
   blessings from above
   And the joy that comes from knowing
   you're safe within His love.
4. *If they counted birthday candles*
   by the thoughtful things you do,
   There'd be about a million
   on a birthday cake for you!

Number one is generally a pretty sendable sentiment.
Number two, however, implies that someone has been having

difficulties that you probably wouldn't bring up in a birthday card. You'd probably find a nice encouragement card if you wanted to address these concerns.

Number three assumes that you have a relationship with the receiver that would allow you to send a religious card. It's not the most generally sendable.

Number four is fairly general, but number one is the most generally sendable. Number four implies a close, ongoing relationship, since the sender is aware of the recipient's good deeds.

EXERCISE 4
Additional or Feature Copy

Freelance writers don't just write me-to-you sentiments; they are often called upon to write a piece for a calendar or plaque or some other product that could stand alone. One popular form answers "What Is a . . . ?" as in "What Is a Husband, Wife, Birthday, etc.?" Here's an example.

What Is a Wife?

A wife is someone
    you can't live without,
She stands close beside you
    day in and day out.
She listens with love
    to the things that you say,
And adds to your joy
    more every day.
A wife is forever,
    the one that you know
Will cherish your dreams
    and help them to grow.

Write a feature verse (either rhymed or prose) that answers the question, "What Is a Wedding?" An example follows.

A wedding is
the celebration
of two hearts
joined in love.
A wedding is
family and friends
sharing the joy
and offering encouragement.
A wedding is
the promise of joy
and commitment
for a lifetime.

EXERCISE 5
Do Your Own Thing

Some card publishers are open to experimental formats and approaches in humor. They welcome cartoons, funny lists, graphs, top tens, and spoofs of movies, TV shows, newspapers, ads and other media. Here's a chance to show just how clever you can be. Write one card of your own using any imaginative approach. If you choose to write to art, clip a picture from a newspaper or magazine and give the punch line.

EXERCISE 6
A Rose by Any Other Name . . .

One of the activities of a writer or editor is naming products to add pizzazz and draw attention to those products. Consider the following products and take a shot at a creative name.

1. A group of cute angel friendship cards

MINE:
Just Winging It!

YOURS:

2. A calendar of puppies and kittens

> MINE:
> *Paws and Whiskers*

> YOURS:

3. A journal for a woman's thoughts

> MINE:
> *Moments of My Own*

> YOURS:

4. A Halloween bat to decorate your door

> MINE:
> *Ding Dong Bat*

> YOURS:

5. An Easter religious boxed card set

> MINE:
> *In His Glory*

> YOURS:

6. An ethnic note card set

> MINE:
> *A World of Love*

> YOURS:

7. A humorous golf card set for Father's Day

MINE:
How to Tee Off Your Dad

YOURS:

A Few More Ways to Practice Your Writing
Brainstorming Techniques
One way to begin brainstorming is to surround yourself with some good magazines and, with your writing topic in mind, try to list as many descriptive words as possible that you might use later when you write your card. For example if your topic is cards for kids, look through a variety of kids magazines and then see what you could do with these words.

bears	kitten
playground	dinosaur
skateboard	circus
funny	tent
swing	doll house
jump rope	monster
french fries	books
hot dogs	

Can you find a picture that spurs an idea for you to write about? Can you relate it to a greeting card? Can you find a way to communicate with a child in a positive way and then find an occasion your card will work for?

Now take each of the words you wrote and see how many you can find a rhyme word for.

bears—cares, stairs, shares, glares, mares, chairs, wears
playground—stay round, way down, greyhound
funny—sunny, honey, runny, punny, money
kitten—mitten, smitten
books—looks, cooks, nooks, hooks, rooks

113

These are just a few of the words, but let's try to write something.

When a bear has no money   (You finish this one.)
but really craves honey
What do you think he should do?

The kitten was smitten   (Your turn.)
with Albert the bear,
She loved his grin
and thick brown hair,
She loved . . .

When birthday girls   (How would you
have a soiree,   finish?)
They plan lots of fun
all through the day,
When birthday boys
have a party too,

You can use this approach with virtually any topic and at least get off the ground or away from a blank page.

Let's try some humorous fall season cards. I'll give you the outside line. You write the inside or the punch line. This is a technique you should practice when you're browsing the card racks.

FRONT:
A Thanksgiving riddle . . .
Why did the chicken cross the road?

INSIDE:
So he could make room for a little pumpkin pie.

FRONT:
What's better than a turkey dressing?

YOUR INSIDE:

FRONT:
Of all the weird things on Halloween . . .

YOUR INSIDE:

Writing Guidelines
The following terms were defined by Hallmark to show what they look for when reviewing portfolios of writers. This is just a partial listing.

Creativity: The talent of being able to bring ideas and concepts to life by using fresh, appealing, dynamic language.

Empathy: The ability to "get into" the minds and hearts of the consumer and weave their feelings into the fabric of the writing.

Grammar: Knowledge of proper usage is a must, even though improper grammar is sometimes used intentionally to enhance the ideas of the card. (Example: Cartoon gangsters saying, "Happy Birthday to YOUSE!")

Originality: The ability to generate new, innovative concepts that are applicable to social expression products.

Passion: The best creative writing samples reflect a passion for the art of writing itself. The reader should be able to feel the joy and exuberance that went into the creation of the piece.

Rhyme & Meter: The ability to craft rhyme and meter effectively and understand the effect different types of rhyme and meter have on verse.

Structure: The element in a piece of writing that sets it apart from routine communication or information. (Examples: a recurring theme in a piece of prose, a specific rhyme scheme in a verse, the correct pacing in a humorous card.)

It's hard to say which of these categories will mean the most to a publisher when you submit your ideas, but it's safe to say that all should be considered seriously before you put your pieces in the mail. You have a lot of competition for the slot your idea might take, so make it the strongest that you can. You'll write the best if you work with passion and have empathy for the consumer. Knowing who you're writing for is key to your sales potential.

A Sample Writing Needs List

- General wishes for birthday
- General age gag
- General slam—pokes fun at the recipient in some way
- Drinking—plays up the celebration aspect of a birthday
- Gift gag—A sentiment about not getting a gift or getting some silly gift.
- Card gag—The focus is on the card itself
- Age-specific birthday—Age 16, 21, 30, 39
- Engagement card—Humorous look at a couple recently engaged
- Good-bye/good luck—Fun ways to say it that haven't been done over and over

Take this sample needs list and try to write at least one card in each of the categories requested. Now, go out to the store and read at least one card in each of the categories. How did your card stack up to the published ones? Were you on target? Were you better? Should you start over?

What Is a Special Assignment?

Sometimes a greeting card publisher will need concept ideas, sentiments or both for a particular project. When that happens, if you have been a frequent freelancer and they have purchased a number of your pieces, they will contact you to help with the project. Here are some sample project possibilities. What would you do with these if you were asked to contribute? Write three ideas for each project.

> **Project 1:** We're looking for humorous woman-to-woman ideas about dating relationships and the difficulty of meeting men to date. Please send any copy ideas that you feel are appropriate. Construction of the verse is open, but we prefer short prose.

> **Project 2:** We're looking for interesting products, both card and non-card, for juvenile Christmas ideas.

Please submit concepts and copy direction for whatever products you develop.

Project 3: We're looking for cards appropriate to the Senior market. Please keep in mind that grandparents range in age from late forties to those well over a hundred. We would like to appeal to those with an active lifestyle.

Direct Mail Companies

Direct mail companies like Current, Inc. in Colorado Springs and Abbey Press in St. Meinrad, Indiana, can be good markets for your writing as well. These companies typically create products directly related to social expression as well as those that are not as clearly defined. They do accept freelance submissions for both card ideas and non-card ideas. Write for guidelines and obtain a recent catalog for an idea of the kind of material they look for.

Here's a tip from Todd Hafer, a writer at Current, Inc.

Catalogs are mailed to general audiences, so your copy cannot be too specific. Very few cards are written for specific relatives. Ninety-eight percent of catalog customers are women. The sentiment becomes even more important when the customer is not able to physically handle the card and see the finishes. Therefore, your writing has to be excellent.

What Help Can I Get From the Internet?

The Internet holds a wealth of information that you may find useful. Publishers of greeting cards offer a variety of ways for you to learn more about writing. Hallmark has an all-inclusive site (http://www.hallmark.com) that shows you everything from greeting cards that you can purchase to historical information about the greeting card industry, to store locations and collectibles. The "funny, but no" section (http://www.shoebox.com/funny/funny.asp) shows you card ideas that were considered funny, but for some reason or other, were not considered strong enough or

117

acceptable as cards to be published. You could learn from this "no" group. Take the lead lines and see if you can make them stronger, or take the suggested theme and see if you can come up with another approach.

The Greet Street site (http://www.greetst.com) shows you hundreds of cards available for purchase—an easy way to do your "shopping" research without stepping a foot outside your door. The more you read what is offered, the better you'll be at guessing what will work when you write your own cards. You cannot, of course, "borrow" ideas, but you can develop your own lines by twisting and turning these ideas in a new direction.

American Greetings has an excellent Web site (http://www .americangreetings.com) that will give you hundreds of leads if you spend some time spinning through the "card rack." You can personalize a card and practice your skills. You might want to stop before you get to the part where you actually purchase a card.

Virtual greeting cards, animated cards, postcards, gifts and alternative forms of greeting card communication abound on the Internet. Whether you need photos to write to, cartoons to help you turn an idea or just great leads, this is a good place to look.

You'll also find information about the Greeting Card Association (GCA) at http://www.greetingcard.org. The GCA can provide you with industry directories and facts, inform you of trends and international trade and legal issues. The majority of greeting card publishers belong to this organization, so this is a good group to be familiar with. You can become a member of the GCA if you'd like.

The Internet can keep you updated about current trends and issues. You can find artists, cartoonists, writers groups, chat groups and others that can assist you in developing your writing skills. Think about starting a newsgroup or Web site yourself to see if you can find others to share your writing interests with.

Developing Your Brainstorming Abilities

If you begin to work on a project for a certain publisher and then get writer's block, here are some ways to look at your topic with fresh insight. Let's pick a topic and apply some brainstorming tools.

Say you have an idea for doing magnet cards for Christmas cards.

- What could you do to make this idea bigger? Could you make the whole card a magnet, make it an ornament or a framed magnet card?
- What if you made the idea smaller? Would mini magnets be a better idea?
- What if you modified the idea? Let's say you wanted magnets in different shapes or formats? Maybe you'd like funny words on them, maybe serious ones?
- Could you rearrange this idea somehow? Could you see it working better for another occasion?
- What about a substitute? What else would work if a magnet didn't? Would stickers or tattoos work?
- What about combining this idea with another one? Maybe a magnet attached to stationery?
- Could you adapt your idea to someone else's idea that you know works already?

Ask "what if" every chance you get. Once you've gotten all your ideas together, give yourself some time and then analyze them. Pick the best ideas and challenge each one. Write your best copy ideas for each.

Here are some topics for you to brainstorm.

- old-time radio shows
- first day of school
- things that are silly
- new love
- favorite desserts for Christmas
- hairstyles
- garage sales
- relatives at Christmas
- types of fathers

Contemporary Topics That Could Benefit Your Writing

1. How might you utilize environmental issues in your writing?
   - recycling
   - ozone layer

- global warming
- saving endangered species

2. How about various roles of men and women today?
    - working moms
    - single dads
    - kids in various stepfamily situations
    - working grandmas
    - dating when you are forty or fifty

3. What about health and fitness issues?
    - jogging grandmas
    - nutrition and eating the right foods
    - watching cholesterol
    - staying active

4. How might you apply a greeting card sentiment to other life issues?
    - women turning fifty or sixty
    - children leaving home
    - baby boomers
    - babies of boomers
    - blended, shrunken, revised, regrouped families
    - kids ages eleven to sixteen
    - taking care of others across the world

5. How might you write for new spiritual awareness?
    - nontraditional Christian/Jewish markets
    - the trends of obvious growth in spiritual awareness
    - beyond New Age thought
    - blending of all kinds of religious philosophy
    - blessed are those . . . (nice format that still works)
    - mind, body, spirit
    - dreams
    - aromatherapy
    - meditation

Greeting card writing today covers a wide range of topics. It has been my hope to help you get started in the business of writing great sentiments and encourage you to find your own niche and your own style. Beyond the traditional card sentiments, you'll find an endless list of contemporary topics. You'll discover that cards reflect the hectic lifestyles of people everywhere. They serve the wonderful purpose of helping people express themselves and create moments to connect to each other in heartfelt ways. I urge you as a writer to really "think outside the box" and go beyond what you've already seen in social expression. You might just hit a strong topic that creates a series and defines a niche that publishers have been waiting for. Be a voice that speaks from the heart or makes someone laugh or brings a moment of cheer. Sometimes the best parts of life are those precious moments we share with people who mean a lot to us. A greeting card can provide that moment. Keep writing! I know you can do it!